SEEDS OF CH

Readings on Cultural Exchange after 1492

A joint project of the
National Museum of Natural History,
Smithsonian Institution,
and the
National Council for the Social Studies

ADDISON-WESLEY PUBLISHING COMPANY
Menlo Park, California • Reading, Massachusetts • New York
Don Mills, Ontario • Wokingham, England • Amsterdam • Bonn
Sydney • Singapore • Tokyo • Madrid • San Juan •Paris
Seoul, Korea • Milan • Mexico City • Taipai, Taiwan

This publication has been made possible through the generous support of The National Potato Board.

The "Seeds of Change" research, exhibitions, publications, and programs have been made possible through the support of the Xerox Corporation. Development of *Seeds of Change* educational materials has been a cooperative venture of the National Museum of Natural History, Smithsonian Institution; Science Weekly, Inc.; and the National Council for the Social Studies.

This book is published by the Addison-Wesley Innovative Division.

Writer/Researcher: Mary Ellen Jones
Contributing Writers: Sue Boulais
                       James E. Davis
                       Sharryl Davis Hawke
Managing Editor: Michael Kane
Project Editor: Priscilla Cox Samii
Design Director: John F. Kelly
Design: Square Moon Productions
Cover Art and Original Artwork: Rachel Gage
Cartography: Krist Mathisen
Composition: Julie Bellitt
Typography: Erin Livers, Arts & Letters
Production Research/Editorial: Leslie Burger

ISBN 0-201-29429-X

1 2 3 4 5 6 7 8 9 10 - XX - 96 95 94 93 92

Contents

To the Student

Dear Student:

Imagine a world without pizza, popcorn, and French fries! Imagine American farms without horses, cows, sheep, or chickens! Such a world existed—500 years ago. In 1492, Christopher Columbus sailed west from Spain in search of the Indies. He found instead two great continents unknown to the peoples of Europe—North and South America.

Columbus began what scholars call "The Columbian Exchange." This refers to the exchange of peoples, animals, plants, and diseases between Europe, Africa, and the Americas that began with Columbus. For example, Columbus and those who followed him brought, among other things, sugarcane, horses, and diseases to America.

The new introductions had an enormous impact on the Americas. Diseases such as smallpox, measles, and the common cold killed thousands of American Indians, who had no immunity to them. Horses, on the other hand, at first frightened the Indians. But, in time, Indians became some of the finest horsemen the world has known.

Sugar, introduced by Columbus on his second voyage, depended upon slavery to make it profitable. Millions of Africans were enslaved to work on the sugar plantations.

From the Americas, Europe, Asia, and Africa received a variety of plants, including the tomato, maize (corn), the potato, tobacco, and quinine. These affected the health and diet of peoples in every corner of the globe.

The book you are about to read, based on the exhibit "Seeds of Change" at the National Museum of Natural History in Washington, D.C., tells this story. The exhibit represents the life's work of scholars from around the world. "Seeds of Change" is their interpretation of the true meaning of Columbus.

Herman J. Viola, Director
Seeds of Change
National Museum of Natural History
Smithsonian Institution

THE ENCOUNTER

A MEETING OF TWO OLD WORLDS

Twenty thousand years ago, immense sheets of ice, called glaciers, stretched across North America from the North Pole to as far south as Mexico. Because much of the earth's water was frozen in the glaciers, sea levels were low and some key areas of land were left uncovered. One area of particular importance to the Americas was a natural land bridge that connected Siberia in northeastern Asia to North America across the Bering Sea.

For thousands of years the land bridge, now the Bering Strait, lay uncovered. During those years, groups of migrant people, as well as animals, traveled across the land bridge. From Asia across to Alaska drifted great mammoths, mastodons, bison with six-foot horns, and rodents the size

of calves. Not far behind came small bands of Ice Age hunters, who depended on the animals for food, clothing, and shelter. The migrants eventually moved into the Americas, some traveling east, some west, and some pushing south through Central America and the South American continent to its southern tip, Tierra del Fuego.

Migration from Asia ended when the Ice Age ended. As the earth warmed, the glaciers melted and sea levels rose. In the north, the rising sea covered the Bering land bridge and separated North America from Asia.

During the 10,000 years that followed, most of the great beasts that had migrated from Asia died out as the climate changed. So did many smaller animals such as the horse.

Keet Seel, a cliff dwelling in Arizona's Canyon de Chelly. Keet Seel dates from the 1200s and was probably occupied by native peoples, called the Anasazi, or "ancient ones."

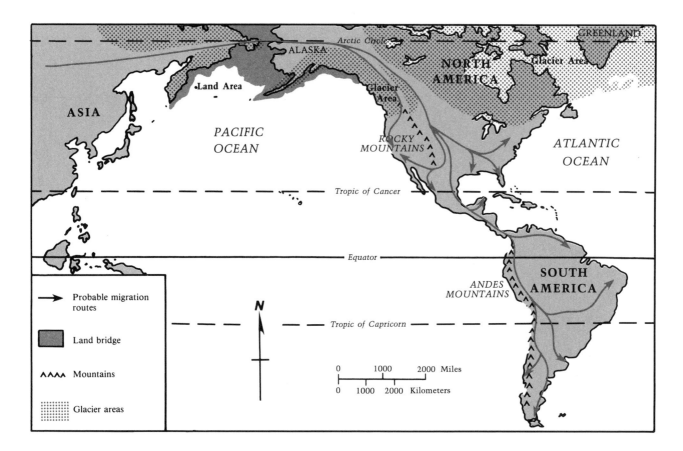

The Bering Land Bridge.
People were able to migrate from Asia to the Americas because lower sea levels during the Ice Age created a temporary strip of land.

The people now isolated in the Americas gradually found or developed other food sources. They continued to explore and settle in new locations as they searched for food. By the end of a hundred centuries, the Americas had become a world of diverse cultures. To a great extent, the cultures that evolved depended on how and where each group obtained its food supply. Some groups depended on hunting and gathering, others on fishing, and others on farming.

Hunters and Gatherers

Following in the footsteps of their Ice Age ancestors, many groups remained nomadic hunters and gatherers. Small family groups banded together to hunt game and gather the nuts, grains, and fruits that grew wild. In the far north, hunter-gatherers traveled the frozen tundras in search of caribou, moose, elk, and deer. In the huge desert basin of present-day Nevada and Utah, hunter-gatherers wandered, looking for seeds, nuts, berries, roots, and insects to eat. They killed small game animals such as birds and rabbits. Hunter-gatherers stalked the buffalo across the

Great Plains. Others ranged through vast South American pampas, looking for wild seeds, fruit, and small game animals such as the rhea, which was similar to the ostrich, or the guanaco, a llama-like animal.

The well-being of each group depended on the success and safety of its hunters. There were no horses, so hunting bands stalked their prey on foot. Working in groups, hunters stampeded animals, especially buffalo, off cliffs or into places where they could be killed easily. Tribes set up temporary camps wherever the location seemed to have a sufficient supply of game and plants, and they changed locations when the food supply dwindled.

Fishing Cultures

Some groups settled along a 2,000-mile stretch of the heavily forested Pacific Northwest coastline. Here the oceans and freshwater streams of the area offered an abundance of fish and other aquatic food sources. The thick forests of giant redwood, Douglas fir, and pine trees provided small game animals, nuts, and berries. In addition, the forests provided a seemingly endless supply of wood to build dwellings and construct large seagoing canoes.

With plentiful supplies of food and building materials, groups in the Pacific Northwest had no need to live a nomadic existence. These peoples settled in villages based on family groups, or clans, and developed rich and complex societies over the centuries. The clans, which were ranked according to wealth and family history, proclaimed their ancestry by carving totem poles to tower in front of their lodges. A totem is an animal or plant symbol associated with a clan. Totem poles became the most visible sign of social status among the peoples of the Northwest.

Farmers

People who were fortunate enough to settle where the climate, soil, and landforms were favorable for growing crops became farmers. Through thousands of growing seasons, these groups progressed from simply gathering wild plants for food and medicine to practicing advanced agriculture. They developed crops that could be planted in the spring and harvested in the fall, as well as crops that could be planted in the fall and harvested in the winter. Most important, the farming groups learned how to purposely crossbreed plants to produce specific growing qualities in their crops. More than 300 kinds of corn were grown in the different soil conditions and climates of the Americas. More than 3,000 kinds of potatoes flourished, especially in Peru. Plants cultivated in the Americas for medicinal purposes numbered over 1,200.

Farming groups usually had much larger populations and settlements than either the fishing clans or the nomadic groups. They developed sophisticated governments and businesses. The Hopewell mound (burial site) builders, for example, dominated the Ohio Valley between 300 B.C. and A.D. 700. They operated a trading system that spanned the North American continent. The desert-dwelling Anasazi extended their influence throughout Arizona, Utah, Colorado, New Mexico, and northern Mexico between 100 B.C. and A.D. 1300. The Anasazi made the deserts bloom with a series of dams, ditches, and canals that almost by magic seemed to increase the area's meager water supply. The northeastern woodland Iroquois built villages of wood-framed longhouses. Sometime during the 1400s, the Iroquois tribes forged one of the first formal peace-keeping alliances in the Americas.

Three Great Empires

The three dominant civilizations that developed in Central and South America—the Mayas, Aztecs, and Incas—were farming cultures. The Mayas ruled in Central America between A.D. 250 and 900. By draining the swamps into an extensive canal system, the Mayas converted the jungles of the Yucatán Peninsula, Guatemala, and Honduras into highly productive farmland. Most Mayan people lived in small villages near cities ruled by chiefs and priests. Cities were religious ceremonial centers consisting of magnificent stone structures such as temple pyramids, astronomical observatories, palaces, public baths, ball courts, plazas, and bridges.

Mayan cities also were centers of art and learning. Mayan artists painted walls with brightly colored murals and created colorful pottery, small clay figures, and huge stone sculptures. Mayan scholars developed intricate mathematical and astronomical systems as well as the only calendar and complete writing system in the Americas.

In the 1300s, the Aztecs came to power in the central valley of Mexico, a huge oval basin about 7,500 feet above sea level. Although the valley was in the tropics, its high altitude gave it a climate milder than that of the surrounding hotter, wetter lowlands.

Like the Mayas, the Aztecs changed the land to make it arable. In the lowlands, they drained marshes, then chopped down and burned sections of forest. They left the ashes to

This Aztec painting tells the story of the Aztecs' migration to the lakes of central Mexico, where they built the city of Tenochtitlán.

act as fertilizer and planted crops in the cleared areas. In the highlands, they cut terraces into the hillsides to increase the amount of level farmland. To water the terraced fields, they dug extensive canals. They turned areas of shallow lakes into croplands by scooping up mud from the lake bottoms to form islands. On these three kinds of farmlands, Aztec farmers grew corn, beans, squash, tomatoes, cotton, cacao, mangoes, papayas, and avocados.

The Aztec capital of Tenochtitlán covered more than ten square miles. Four hundred thousand residents bustled through its streets. Canals and causeways connected the capital to nearby cities and villages. Tenochtitlán's administrative center contained law courts, a jail, a military academy, a public treasury, and living quarters for 3,000 servants and workers.

In Aztec marketplaces people traded gold, silver, precious gems, feathers, embroidered goods, building supplies, and foods of all kinds. The abundance of goods was a result of tributes from conquered peoples and a trading system that reached throughout Mexico.

In South America, the empire of the Incas stretched along about 2,000 miles of the rugged terrain of the Andes Mountains. This vast empire had expanded between about A.D. 1400 and 1500 and included southern Colombia, Ecuador, Peru, Bolivia, and parts of Chile and Argentina. Inca farmers living in the small valleys of the Andean mountains dug irrigation ditches and hillside terraces in the surrounding slopes. Inca farms became so efficient that they produced enough corn and potatoes to fill thousands of storehouses holding as much as seven years' worth of food.

The Inca empire was made up of conquered peoples from the west coast of South America. To hold their empire together, the Incas constructed a road system that covered more than 25,000 miles of steep mountains and ravines. Along the roads, runners sped to transmit news, imperial troops marched to quell uprisings, and traders traveled to and from Chile, Argentina, and Ecuador.

Cultures of the Americas

Methods of obtaining food—whether by hunting and gathering, fishing, or farming—led to differences in social structures, religion, ceremonies, art, and medicine. Other differences among early American peoples developed as groups

Incas used the quipu, *an abacus-like device, to calculate the tribute owed them by conquered peoples.*

adapted to the climates of their chosen environments. Those living in the coldest northern climates made protective clothing from seal or caribou skin and built dome-shaped homes of earthen or snow blocks. Groups that settled in dense northeastern forests used deer hides both to make clothing and to cover the log frames of their wigwams. Plains groups hunted the buffalo and left no part of that animal unused. Desert dwellers built apartment-like pueblos with thick adobe walls that kept the interiors cool.

In spite of their many differences, these diverse peoples shared some common beliefs. Most believed in a creator. They also believed in a sacred relationship between humans and nature. According to this belief, each individual shared the task of maintaining the balance of nature, and whatever was taken from the land was used wisely.

By the late 1400s, the Americas were populated from the Arctic to the Andes with differing, complex cultures. Most of these cultures had not had much negative impact on their environments, nor had they damaged significantly the *ecosystem*, the delicate balance among land, plants, and animals. All had developed without the horse or any other large, tamed beasts of burden. They had been isolated and protected from epidemic diseases and plagues.

The world of the early Americans was about to change. Sailing toward them were three small ships from the other side of the globe. The captain was a determined Italian sailor under the patronage of the Spanish king and queen.

European Exploration and the Search for the Indies

In the late 1400s, four nations—Spain, Portugal, France, and England—were vying for European leadership. Heads of these nations were searching for ways to increase their countries' wealth and power. One way, they believed, was to expand trade with the Indies—the Asian lands of China, Japan, Indonesia, and India.

Europeans knew little about the Indies, but they did know about products from that part of the world. Gold, pepper, ginger, cloves, perfumes, silks, and other riches were brought to Mediterranean markets by Venetian traders. Indies trade, however, was controlled by Venetian, Asian, and Arab merchants, who were able to make handsome profits by controlling the trade. Finding new trade routes to the Indies would help European countries establish direct trade and thereby gain more profits. Europe's monarchs began to support voyages of exploration to find new sea routes to the Indies.

Recent inventions such as the compass and the astrolabe made the navigation of such voyages more accurate and thus safer. Triangular sails and the replacement of steering oars with a rudder changed the look and performance of seagoing vessels. The sails made better use of sea winds. The rudder, a hinged piece of wood attached to the ship's stern, or rear, allowed more control in steering.

Explorers who claimed lands and established settlements for a country received honors and money from the government. Christopher Columbus, an Italian sea captain, wanted such recognition. For seven years prior to 1492, Columbus had haunted the Spanish courts of King Ferdinand and Queen Isabella, trying to persuade them to finance an expedition that would find the Indies by sailing west. Isabella, eager to expand Spanish influence, was sympathetic to Columbus, but at first Ferdinand was not. In 1492, however, Spain's war against Moors (Moslems) in the south ended when Spanish imperial troops defeated the Moors. Ferdinand was filled with religious fervor against Moslems, including the Arabs who controlled trade with the Indies. He and Isabella outfitted Columbus with supplies and three ships, the *Niña*, the *Pinta*, and the *Santa María*.

On August 3, 1492, Christopher Columbus set sail from Palos, Spain, for "God, glory, and gold." He wanted converts to Christianity, glory for himself, and gold for Spain.

The First Encounter

More than two months later, Columbus and his ships were still sailing west. There had been no sight of land since the ships had left the Canary Islands off the northwest coast of Africa. The men were ready to mutiny. Their salted meat and dried beans were almost gone, and the biscuits were infested with maggots. The crew was bored, restless, and beginning to fear they were lost.

On October 10, Columbus had bargained with them to sail three more days. If they did not sight land by then, he promised they would return to Spain. At 2:00 A.M. on the third day, pacing the deck of the *Santa María*, Columbus heard the lookout sailor from the *Pinta* shout, "Land! Land!" To prevent the ships from running aground, Columbus

Columbus and later European explorers were able to sail across oceans because of navigational equipment such as the compass and the astrolabe.

SEEDS • OF • CHANGE

ordered each one to lower its sails and drop anchor. With the first dawn light, the ships edged toward land.

As they approached, Columbus realized that the large land mass he had been expecting was instead a small island. As he was familiar with the writings of earlier explorers, however, he wasn't concerned. He believed there were many small islands offshore from the Indies.

Finding a place to drop anchor, Columbus and the captains from the *Niña* and the *Pinta* took rowboats ashore. Their first act on land that morning of October 12, 1492, was to kneel and thank their Christian God for allowing the ships to reach land. Columbus then planted the Spanish flag in the sandy soil and claimed the island for Ferdinand and Isabella. He named it *San Salvador*, which means "Holy Savior." Later he greeted the island's people, the Arawaks.

The meeting between Columbus and the Arawaks brought together two worlds that had been isolated from one another for 10,000 years. The period of European conquest and colonization of the Americas had begun.

Naming the Indies
Columbus was certain he had found a gateway to the East Indies. Instead, he had bumped into islands that are part of the Bahamas chain. The Bahamas lie between the Atlantic Ocean and the Caribbean Sea, south of present-day Florida. Both the islands and their inhabitants were misnamed. Even when Columbus's mistake was discovered, the islands retained the name of *Indies*. The word "West" was added so they would not be confused with the other "East" Indies. The islands' inhabitants continued to be called "Indians," a name that was applied to all peoples on the American continents.

Two days after his landing on San Salvador, Columbus and some crew members explored the rest of the island, then sailed to other islands nearby. Hoping to find gold, gems, or spices, they found instead peaceful people and an astonishing array of unfamiliar animals and plants. "I believe the islands contain many herbs and many trees which will be worth a great amount in Spain for dyes and as medicinal spices, but I do not recognize them and I much regret that," wrote Columbus in his journal.

Columbus returned to Spain without having found vast amounts of gold or gems. He did, however, bring back six

The Niña *was Columbus's favorite ship. Columbus credited the sturdy* Niña *for the safe journey home on his first voyage.*

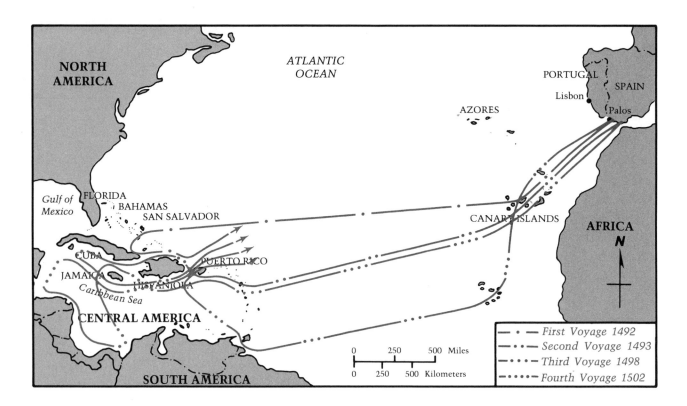

NORTH AMERICA

ATLANTIC OCEAN

PORTUGAL
Lisbon
SPAIN
Palos

AZORES

FLORIDA
Gulf of Mexico
BAHAMAS
SAN SALVADOR

CANARY ISLANDS

AFRICA
N

CUBA
JAMAICA
HISPANIOLA
PUERTO RICO
Caribbean Sea

CENTRAL AMERICA

SOUTH AMERICA

| 0 | 250 | 500 Miles |
| 0 | 250 | 500 Kilometers |

— ·— First Voyage 1492
— · ·— Second Voyage 1493
— · · ·— Third Voyage 1498
— · · · ·— Fourth Voyage 1502

***The Four Voyages of
Columbus to the Americas***

"Indian" captives to prove his claim that he had reached
the Indies. He hoped his evidence would convince the
Spanish monarchs to provide funds for a second voyage.

European Misperceptions of the Americas

Columbus managed to obtain funding not only for a second voyage but for a third and a fourth, as well. Meanwhile,
other navigators had begun sailing across the Atlantic to the
Americas. In the twelve years following 1492, more than
eighty exploration voyages reached the Americas. Because
they made little or no effort to understand the land or the
peoples of the Americas, the early explorers formed false or
inaccurate ideas about the American Indians and their lands.
Most Europeans came to believe these misperceptions.

The first misperception was the idea that the Americas
were a "new world." To Columbus and the Europeans, the
two huge land masses may have been new. But to the peoples living there, the Americas were as old as Europe was to
Columbus and other Europeans.

Another misperception was that Europeans had "discovered" the Americas. Columbus had encountered lands yet
unexplored by Europeans. Early Americans had already

SEEDS • OF • CHANGE

"discovered" and explored nearly all the land of the two vast continents centuries before the Europeans arrived.

The third misperception was that land in the Americas was unsettled, unlimited, and free for the taking. To Europeans, settled land was owned and fenced off by individuals. The concepts of fences, boundaries, and private land ownership did not exist for American Indians. To them, settled land was any land they used.

Europeans quickly extended the misperceptions of "undiscovered" and "free for the taking" to include all of the Americas' natural resources. American Indians, for the most part, used only what they needed from their world's abundant game animals, rich forests, and mineral wealth of gold, silver, copper, and tin. They did not damage or destroy natural resources for the purpose of gaining wealth.

The greatest and perhaps most damaging misperception fostered by the early explorers was the belief that the peoples of the Americas were uncivilized. Columbus's first descriptions of the Arawaks reflected his belief that they could be easily conquered. He noted that they "bore no arms, nor knew of them . . . had no iron . . . and went around as naked as the days their mothers bore them."

He reasoned that armed men should be able to enslave them easily and make them do "whatever one might wish." He thought their gentleness would also make it easy to convert them to Christianity. He wrote, "Christendom will do good business with these Indians, especially Spain, whose subjects they must all become." Looking back, this statement was a sad forecast of the future. For soon, Spanish adventurers, called *conquistadors,* would conquer large areas of the Americas and enslave thousands of Indians. Later, both North and South America would become colonized by people of many different European countries.

The Americas' First Environmentalists

What the Europeans did not recognize, and what we are now only beginning to understand fully, is how advanced many American Indian groups were 500 years ago. The Aztecs and Mayas had built astounding structures because of their knowledge of advanced mathematics and physics. American Indians had developed solar calendars much more accurate than European calendars. American Indian farmers grew a wide variety of food plants, thanks to careful

Present-day White Mountain Apaches make a ritual climb up Sacred Mountain to give thanks for the land.

recording of weather patterns and soil conditions. They also developed new crops and natural medicines.

American Indians had ongoing traditions of family and community life. Most had strong family ties, with parents and grandparents serving as children's teachers. Family and community histories were passed down through storytelling and drawings on cave walls, hides, pottery, and woven cloth.

Today we admire the Indians' knowledge of and respect for nature. Present-day scientists are trying to learn what the Indians 500 years ago already knew about conserving the land and natural resources. As we attempt to save the earth's natural environment today, we would do well to remember the Indians as the Americas' first environmentalists.

The Exchanges Begin

On his second voyage to the Americas, Columbus brought seventeen ships filled with European settlers, plants, and animals. He landed on the island that he had named *Hispaniola*, "Little Spain," and unloaded his ships. The exchanges that would change the entire world began.

Columbus's crew members planted seeds and cuttings, introducing into the Americas wheat, melons, onions, lettuce, grapes, and sugarcane. With the exception of sugarcane, these plants did not thrive well in the tropical areas of the Caribbean, although later many would grow very successfully in other parts of the Americas.

Animals that were unloaded included pigs, cattle, chickens, sheep, goats, and a true native American returning home—the horse. Unlike the plants, the animals did well in the tropics, where there was endless natural feed and no animal-killing diseases. Within thirty years, the animal herds had multiplied many times over.

Columbus and his crew also brought a silent but deadly European export—disease. Within several days of the Europeans' landing, hundreds of Hispaniola islanders had caught a fatal respiratory disease. Contagious diseases were common in Europe, but the native populations of the Americas had never been exposed to them and had not developed immunities.

Five Powerful Exchanges

Columbus's accidental landing in the Americas did not fulfill his dreams. He never found the gold he sought, and he enjoyed fame and royal favor for only a short time. But his encounter with the Americas set off the most powerful plant, animal, disease, and cultural exchanges in history.

The sugarcane that Columbus brought to Hispaniola would eventually introduce the plantation system, lead to the use of slave labor, and begin the assault on the earth's tropical forests. The horse that Columbus returned to its native homeland would first frighten the American Indians and then alter their way of life. The diseases that Columbus unwittingly turned loose on the unsuspecting, unprepared native American population would kill between 50 and 90 percent of those peoples. Corn from American Indians' fields would be introduced to Europe and Africa and would feed the enslaved Africans who provided the labor for American plantations. The potato, another American Indian crop, would, like corn, become a worldwide staple after its introduction into Europe.

In the next five chapters, you will learn how the Columbus encounter began a series of long-lasting and powerful exchanges between two old worlds. You will discover how five "seeds of change" planted 500 years ago have influenced the lives of people throughout the world, and will continue to have influence worldwide.

DISEASE
AN ALLY IN CONQUEST

The first European seed of change planted in the Americas was *infectious disease.* Silently, invisibly, and immediately, infectious diseases took root in the Americas. These were sicknesses that spread from person to person through the air, by human touch, on clothing, and in food and water. *Epidemics* of these diseases swept through the Americas, moving swiftly from village to village, striking down entire populations of American Indians.

To American Indians the diseases were unknown. They seemed to have no cause, and they certainly had no cure. There were no vaccinations in 1492, no wonder drugs. Measles, mumps, typhus, and diphtheria infected and killed many American Indians. One European disease was more

deadly than the rest. Smallpox killed millions of American Indians and paved the way for easy conquest by Europeans.

The Killer Pox

Smallpox was highly contagious. Victims became infected by breathing in germs or touching infected persons. There were no signs of illness until about the ninth day, when the person experienced headaches, backaches, fever, chills, nausea, and sometimes convulsions and delirium. Three or four days later, the fever dropped and the victim felt better. But the break was only temporary. The virus then came out in the open, producing its characteristic rash of flat, reddish spots. The fever returned and the rash spread

This woodcut depicts mortal illness among the Wampanoag Indians in Massachusetts shortly after the arrival of the first settlers from England in the 1620s.

from the face to the rest of the body. During the next several days, the victim became a horrendous, swollen "monster" as the flat spots raised into pimples, then turned into blisters filled with pus. If the person continued to live, the blisters broke, the pus dried, and the sores turned into crusts or scabs. Most survivors had scars, or pockmarks, from the disease.

Many smallpox victims died during the first few days of the rash. Some died even before the rash appeared. Once a person was infected, there was no effective treatment. Even death did not stop the disease. Pus from the rash or scabs from the dried sores contaminated blankets and clothing.

Europe's Long History of Diseases
Europeans had long had contact with smallpox and many other infectious diseases. By the time Columbus reached the Americas, Europeans had been exploring, trading, and warring on their own continent for several centuries. Travelers to Asia and Africa were exposed to diseases common there and unknowingly brought them back to Europe. Epidemics followed as the illnesses quickly spread through the crowded cities of Europe.

Contagious diseases hit children the hardest. Only one child in two had a chance of living to age fifteen. However, those who survived developed an immunity to these diseases and could not be infected again. Through years of epidemics, Europeans built up immunities to a wide range of infectious diseases.

The Isolated Americas
American Indians had no protection from European sicknesses. There were no infectious diseases of epidemic proportions in the Americas before Columbus landed. American Indians had not developed immunities to European diseases.

Several conditions explained the lack of infectious epidemics in the Americas. First, if early migrants brought diseases with them across the Bering land bridge, those who were ill probably didn't survive the journey. Second, the cold climate of the migration route may have kept disease germs from surviving. Finally, American Indian groups' isolation from each other reduced the likelihood of epidemics. Although these conditions kept people of the Americas free of epidemics, they also prevented American Indians from developing immunities.

The Americas weren't disease free, however, or without health difficulties. Almost all groups had some form of intestinal worms, and most had dental problems. Some suffered from tuberculosis or other respiratory diseases. Ironically, peoples who developed highly sophisticated agricultural societies with large, permanent settlements often had poor health. As in Europe, the cities and towns of the early Americas had polluted water supplies. More than likely, they also had inadequate sanitation and waste-disposal systems. These American communities had some infectious disease, but it was confined to individual sites.

American Indians had developed an extensive array of plant-derived remedies for many illnesses. They had quinine to cure malaria, ipecac to induce vomiting, a kind of aspirin for headaches, and herbal teas for sore throats. Aztec doctors used more than 1,200 plants to treat specific diseases. Several American Indian groups practiced sophisticated surgical techniques. In addition, American Indians bathed daily to rid themselves of dirt on their bodies on which germs might multiply.

By contrast, Europeans of the time bathed infrequently, their herbal knowledge was limited, and bloodletting and prayer were their primary medicinal treatments. Barber-surgeons cut hair, amputated limbs, and pulled teeth.

European Diseases Arrive

No amount of plant remedies, bathing, or surgical practices prepared American Indians for the silent deadliness of infectious disease from Europe. Many of the Arawaks who met Columbus died within weeks from a respiratory disease they caught from the sailors. As more Europeans came to the Americas, more diseases came, too. Smallpox arrived in 1518 on Hispaniola, the island where the Spanish had begun their first colony. An early Spanish historian of the Americas estimated that a million Indians lived on the island in 1518. Thirty years later, fewer than a thousand were left.

Soon after the disease began to decimate the Arawaks on Hispaniola, the "dreaded pox" attacked Puerto Rico to the east and moved west into Haiti. It advanced relentlessly through Haiti and then Cuba, and hit the Yucatán

Vase from the Chicama Valley of Peru showing facial scabs and sores, probably from smallpox.

Peninsula of southern Mexico in 1519. By 1520, smallpox had begun its assault on the Aztecs. It served as an ally to Spanish conquistador Hernán Cortés in the conquest of the great Aztec empire in central Mexico.

Disease Conquers the Mainland

In 1519, Cortés and about 500 soldiers and 16 horses marched into the Aztec capital of Tenochtitlán. Mistaken for gods and offered Aztec wealth and friendship by the Aztec leader, Montezuma II, the Spaniards captured the sprawling, magnificent city and eventually enslaved the Aztecs for "God, glory, and gold."

On July 1, 1520, the Aztecs revolted, and the Spanish were forced to fight their way out of the city and flee. As the Spanish left, smallpox entered. By the time Cortés returned to counterattack, the disease had infected the Aztec population and fighting force of more than one million people. The Spaniards besieged Tenochtitlán for 75 days before it fell in August 1521.

The smallpox virus struck out along South American trade routes. Borne on the air, it contaminated traders as well as their goods. It traveled swiftly into both heavily populated cities and small villages. Often, the disease arrived before the conquerors, making their task much easier. In 1531, Spanish explorer Francisco Pizarro led his soldiers into Inca territory in Peru. He found that the great Inca ruler, Huayna Capac, and his military leaders, along with thousands of Inca people, had died, "their faces covered with scabs." Pizarro easily took over.

Smallpox decimated the native peoples in North America as well. The disease spread from tribe to tribe through trade and wars. Journals of English, French, and Spanish explorers during the 1500s and 1600s carried reports of Indian villages peopled only with scabbed dead bodies. In 1731, Blackfoot Indian scouts came across a Shoshone tribe's village in what is now the western United States. All the Shoshone were dead in their tepees. The Blackfoot scouts returned home with items from the village, not knowing they also had brought smallpox with them. Within weeks, two-thirds of the Blackfoot were dead.

Infectious diseases, led by smallpox, had their worst impact during the first 100 years after the Europeans' arrival. Repeated epidemics almost totally destroyed some American

Indian groups and greatly reduced others. Their resistance to disease was lowered by the brutal treatment most enslaved Indians received from their European masters. Experts estimate that 50 to 90 percent of the American Indian population was killed by infectious diseases between 1500 and 1900.

The conquistadors' brutality contributed to disease and death among the enslaved Aztecs.

The Syphilis Exchange

The introduction of disease was not all one way. Shortly after Columbus and his crew returned from the Americas, an epidemic of venereal disease spread throughout Europe. This particular strain, which came to be known as *syphilis*, is not known to have been described in Europe before Columbus's initial voyage. In addition, American Indian skeletons before 1492 show signs characteristic of syphilis, while European skeletons do not. Did Columbus and his crew bring syphilis back to Europe? Given the fact that so many diseases traveled to the Americas from Europe and Africa, it wouldn't be surprising if some native American sicknesses traveled back. Syphilis may have been one of them.

Never-Ending Disease

A vaccine to prevent massive smallpox epidemics did not appear until 1796. The disease was not conquered until 1980, when the World Health Organization declared that it had been eliminated worldwide. The end of smallpox, however, has not meant the end of deadly infectious disease in the world. In the same year that smallpox was laid to rest, a new virus appeared—AIDS (Acquired Immune Deficiency Syndrome). Today, this deadly virus has no known cure.

In searching for a cure to AIDS and other diseases, contemporary scientists are taking a cue from the Americas' early inhabitants. They are investigating plant species from the world's tropical rain forests for medicinal compounds that may be useful in the treatment of AIDS, cancer, and other diseases.

How might life be different today if the American Indians had not contracted smallpox and other infectious diseases the Europeans brought with them? How might history have been different if the Europeans had been met by the full strength of the American Indians? The answers to these questions will never be known. However, we can be sure that the Americas today would be significantly different if disease had not become an ally in conquest.

The Conquest of Smallpox

By the late 1700s it was commonly known that a person could catch smallpox only once. Even a mild case of the disease would give a person immunity for life.

British doctor Edward Jenner learned that cowpox, a disease similar to smallpox, caused a few sores on the hands of those who worked with cattle but did not result in death or disfiguring sores all over the body. Dr. Jenner predicted that someone who had had cowpox might be immune to smallpox. To test his idea, he infected a healthy boy with cowpox and several weeks later infected the same boy with smallpox. The boy did not get smallpox. Dr. Jenner had *vaccinated* the boy with cowpox against smallpox!

After more vaccination experiments, Dr. Jenner made his discovery known in 1798. Through mass vaccinations, smallpox has become the first major infectious disease to be wiped out worldwide.

Vaccinating patients with cowpox.

HEALTH PROFILES

John W. Verano and Douglas H. Ubelaker

According to some reports, American Indians generally were in better health than the Spanish conquistadors. These health profiles of an Aztec warrior and a Spanish conquistador were written by scholars at the National Museum of Natural History, Smithsonian Institution.

An Aztec Warrior

In Aztec society, success on the battlefield was a principal vehicle for social advancement, and most young men were eager to become warriors. The battlefield was a hazardous place, however. . . . To treat its wounded the Aztec army maintained specialists who set fractured bones, realigned dislocated joints, and cleansed and sutured lacerations.

Common health complaints included intestinal disorders, headaches, coughs, and fevers. It was widely believed that disease was sent by the gods or was the result of sorcery, hence the advice of a professional healer was often sought—both to cure a disease and to divine its source. There were many healers in Aztec society who specialized in particular ailments, and treatment frequently combined ritual activities and herbal remedies. Some twelve hundred plants were used by the Aztecs for medicinal purposes. Most of these plants and plant preparations could be purchased in the marketplace from a vendor who specialized in herbs, medicines, and curing paraphernalia.

The Aztec people were meticulous about personal hygiene. They bathed regularly in streams and lakes, and took frequent sweat baths as well. Most dwellings in Tenochtitlán had a bathhouse, a small, circular structure that was heated by a fire built against the outer wall. The bather entered the structure and threw water against the wall to produce steam. Steam baths were used for personal cleaning, as well as to treat coughs, fevers, and joint problems. The Aztecs also recognized the importance of dental hygiene and cleaned their teeth regularly with powdered charcoal and salt. . . .

A Spanish Conquistador

The Spanish conquistadores who made their way to the New World were survivors of a long and harsh process of selection. Infant mortality was high in fifteenth- and sixteenth-century Europe. One out of every three children died in the first year, and less than half survived to age fifteen. Poor nutrition and infectious disease were major contributors to this high mortality. Vitamin deficiencies were common, and scurvy was a familiar companion of sea voyagers. Recurrent outbreaks of bubonic plague, smallpox, measles, typhus, and other infectious diseases periodically winnowed the population of Europe, as did drought and famine. In terms of personal hygiene, the Spanish conquistador had much to learn from his Aztec adversary. Bathing was a seldom-practiced ritual in sixteenth-century Europe, and cities of this period were not renowned for their sanitary conditions.

While Europeans had a vague notion of the contagious nature of some diseases, illness more commonly was attributed to astrological phenomena, curses, personal and moral dissoluteness, and, above all, divine retribution upon sinful man. Medical treatments, which might include bleeding of the patient and treatment with herbal remedies, were aimed at restoring the balance of bodily humors—blood, phlegm, yellow bile, and black bile. While a wealthy individual might consult a university-trained physician for treatment of an illness, the common man generally relied on barber-surgeons, apothecaries, and self-taught practitioners. Barber-surgeons were the medical personnel who accompanied the Spanish conquistadores and early colonists to the New World. A general lack of confidence in their medical skill is suggested by the fact that conquistadores frequently sought out Aztec practitioners for health complaints, in preference to their fellow countrymen.

The Spanish who came to the New World in the early sixteenth century were tough, wiry, battle-scarred adventurers. Many showed the characteristic pockmarks left by a bout with smallpox during childhood, as well as wounds sustained in previous military campaigns. While they had little understanding of how to protect their health or to treat their illnesses, they were survivors, nevertheless. And like their Aztec opponents on the battlefield, they had little fear of death.

THE PLAGUE
RAVAGES THE CITY

It took nearly two years for Cortés to topple the Aztec empire in Mexico. The defeat of the Aztecs was not the result of superior Spanish military strength, however. Smallpox was the invisible ally of the Spanish in the conquest. A smallpox epidemic ravaged the Aztec population in early 1521. By spring, the Aztec population was defenseless against the siege on Tenochtitlán. When the victorious Spaniards entered the city, one historian wrote, "the streets, squares, houses, and courts were filled with bodies, so that it was almost impossible to pass. Even Cortés was sick from the stench." The short reading that follows is a modern translation of an Aztec account of the effects of smallpox on the city.

While the Spaniards were in Tlaxcala,* a great plague broke out here in Tenochtitlán. It began to spread during the thirteenth month and lasted for seventy days, striking everywhere in the city and killing a vast number of our people. Sores erupted on our faces, our breasts, our bellies; we were covered with agonizing sores from head to foot.

The illness was so dreadful that no one could walk or move. The sick were so utterly helpless that they could only lie on their beds like corpses, unable to move their limbs or even their heads. They could not lie face down or roll from one side to the other. If they did move their bodies, they screamed with pain.

A great many died from this plague, and many others died of hunger. They could not get up to search for food, and everyone else was too sick to care for them, so they starved to death in their beds. Some people came down with a milder form of the disease; they suffered less than the others and made a good

As you read:
• As smallpox killed hundreds of thousands of Aztecs, what do you think might have happened to the morale of Aztec warriors?

*The city to which Cortés retreated after the Aztec revolt in Tenochtitlán.

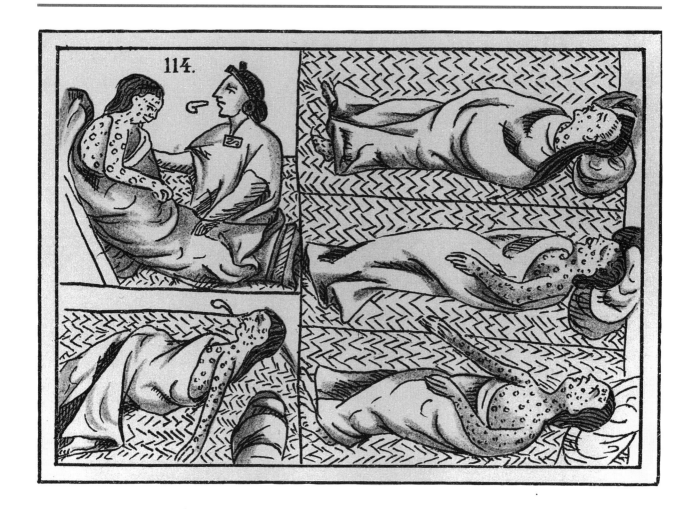

Picture from an Aztec codex, or illustrated history, showing the progression of smallpox in a victim.

recovery. But they could not escape entirely. Their looks were ravaged, for wherever a sore broke out, it gouged an ugly pockmark in the skin. And a few of the survivors were left completely blind.

The first cases were reported in Cuatlan. By the time the danger was recognized, the plague was so well established that nothing could halt it, and eventually it spread all the way to Chalco. Then its virulence [infectiousness] diminished considerably, though there were isolated cases for many months after. The first victims were stricken during the fiesta of Teotleco, and the faces of our warriors were not clean and free of sores until the fiesta of Panquetzaliztli.

CONQUISTADORS AND DISEASE

~

Alfred W. Crosby, Jr.

Alfred W. Crosby, Jr., is a professor of American Studies at the University of Texas, Austin. He is an internationally recognized expert on the biological exchanges that resulted from Columbus's voyages. In the following excerpt from his book The Columbian Exchange, *Dr. Crosby summarizes the effects of European diseases on the Indians of the Americas.*

The record of early post-Columbian medical history of America was never kept carefully and much of it has been erased since, but it does seem to show a greater number of epidemics, characterized by a higher mortality rate, than was typical even in insalubrious [not healthful] Europe of that time. The very first was a pandemic [widespread epidemic] which began in 1519 in the Greater Antilles and swept through Mexico, Central America, and—probably—Peru. It caused "in all likelihood the most severe single loss of aboriginal [native] population that ever occurred," to quote one expert who has examined its history carefully.[1]* It is the best documented of all of the first epidemics. We have no more than snatches of information on the others. . . . In 1558 pleurisy [respiratory inflammation] and bloody flux [diarrhea] spread along the coast from Río [de Janeiro] to Espírito Santo. In 1558 and 1560 smallpox arrived in Río de la Plata and swept off thousands of Indians, without touching a single Spaniard. Smallpox came to Brazil in 1562 and 1563 and carried off tens of thousands of Indians, but left the Portuguese unscathed. In some villages no one was left who was healthy enough to tend the sick, "not even someone who could go to the fountain for a gourdfull of water."[2]

The English were as efficient disease carriers as the Latins. In 1585 Sir Francis Drake led a large expedition against Spain's

---

*Numbers refer to Readings Notes on page 123.

As you read:
- What do you conclude about the European attitudes toward American Indian deaths from disease?
- Whom did the Indians blame for their sickness and death?

CHAPTER 2 • DISEASE

29

overseas possessions. His men picked up some highly contagious fever—probably typhus—in the Cape Verde Islands and brought it along with them to the Caribbean and Florida. The malady spread to the Indians in the environs of St. Augustine and, "The wilde people . . . died verie fast and said amongest themselves, it was the Inglisshe God that made them die so faste."[3] . . .

The natives of what is now the Atlantic coast of Canada had contact with Europeans—fishermen and fur traders—from very early in the sixteenth century, long before the English attempted colonization at Roanoke or any other place in America. Depopulation was already apparent among their tribes by the time of French settlement. The Jesuit *Relations* contain a report dated 1616 from which the following paragraph is extracted. The Indians, it states,

> *are astonished and often complain that, since the French mingle with and carry on trade with them, they are dying fast and the population is thinning out. For they assert that, before this association . . . all their countries were very populous and they tell how one by one the different coasts, according as they have begun to traffic with us, have been more reduced by disease.[4]*

These Indians looked south enviously to New England, where tribes were not diminishing. The turn of these Armouchiquois, as the Canadian Indians called them, came in the same year that the above report was written. In 1616 and 1617 a pestilence [epidemic] swept through New England, clearing the woods, in the words of Cotton Mather,* "of those pernicious [wicked] creatures, to make room for better growth." Whatever the sickness was, Europeans were immune to it. The handful of whites who passed the winter of 1616–1617 with the Indians of coastal Maine "lay in the cabins with those people that died, [but] not one of them ever felt their heads to ache, while they stayed there." The Massachusetts tribe was nearly completely exterminated, depopulating the area of Plymouth Bay at just about the same time that the Pilgrims were deciding to come to America. The same epidemic also swept the environs of Boston Bay. A European who lived in that area in 1622 wrote that the Indians had

The results of smallpox show on Running Face, a member of the Mandan tribe, who survived the 1837 epidemic.

---

*Cotton Mather (1663–1728) was a Puritan minister, writer, and community leader in Boston.

SEEDS • OF • CHANGE

died on heapes, as they lay in their houses; and the living, that were able to shift for themselves, would runne away and let them dy, and let there Carkases ly above the ground without burial. . . . And the bones and skulls upon the severall places of their habitations made such a specta-cle after my coming into those partes, that, as I travailed in the Forrest nere the Massachusetts, it seemed to me a new found Golgotha [Calvary—site of Jesus' crucifixion; a place of agony].[5]

There is no need to continue this lugubrious [sad] catalog. The records of every European people who have had prolonged contact with the native peoples of America are full of refer-ences to the devastating impact of Old World diseases. The Russians, the last to come, had the same experience as the Spanish, Portuguese, English, and French; and thousands of Aleuts, Eskimos, and Tlingits were thrust into their graves by the maladies which the promyshlenniki [Russian trappers and traders]—as innocent of intent as the conquistadores—brought to the New World with them.[6]

Sickness Comes with You

Chiparopai, an old Yuma Indian, gives her views of the changes that confronted her at the beginning of the twenti-eth century.

Sickness comes with you [the White Man] and hundreds of us die. Where is our strength? . . . In the old times we were strong. We used to hunt and fish. We raised our little crop of corn and melons and ate the mesquite beans. Now all is changed. . . . Each day in the old times in summer and in winter we came down to the river banks to bathe. This strengthened and toughened our firm skin. But white settlers were shocked to see the naked Indians, so now we keep away. In old days we wore the breechcloth, and aprons made of bark and reeds. We worked all winter in the wind—bare arms, bare legs, and never felt the cold. But now, when the wind blows down from the mountains it makes us cough. Yes—we know that when you come, we die.

HISTORY OF THE PLYMOUTH PLANTATION

William Bradford

William Bradford, who completed History of the Plymouth Plantation *in 1650, was the second governor of the Plymouth Colony in present-day Massachusetts. The following passage from Bradford's book describes a smallpox epidemic among the Narragansett Indians who lived near Plymouth Colony.*

This spring also, those Indians that lived about their trading house there, fell sick of the small pox and died most miserably. . . . For usually they that have this disease have them in abundance, and for want of bedding and linen and other helps they fall into a lamentable condition as they lie on their hard mats, the pox breaking and mattering and running one into another, their skin cleaving by reason thereof to the mats they lie on. When they turn them, a whole side will flay off at once as it were, and they will be all of a gore blood, most fearful to behold. . . . The condition of this people was so lamentable and they fell down so generally of this disease as they were in the end not able to help one another, no not to make a fire nor to fetch a little water to drink, nor any to bury the dead. But would strive as long as they could, and when they could procure no other means to make fire, they would burn the wooden trays and dishes they ate their meat in, and their very bows and arrows. And some would crawl out on all fours to get a little water, and sometimes die by the way and not be able to get in again. But of those of the English house [Plymouth colonists], though at first they were afraid of the infection, yet seeing their woeful and sad condition and hearing their pitiful cries and lamentations, they had compassion on them, and daily fetched them wood and water and made them fires, got them victuals [food] whilst they lived; and buried them when they died. For very few of them escaped, notwithstanding they did what they could for them to the hazard of themselves.

I HAVE SPOKEN

Four Bears

In 1837 the Mandan tribe that lived near present-day Bismarck, North Dakota, almost vanished as a result of a smallpox epidemic. Four Bears, called Ma-to-toh-pah, second chief of the Mandans, spoke to his people on July 30, 1837, the day he died of the disease. A trader recorded his speech.

My Friends one and all, Listen to what I have to say—Ever since I can remember, I have loved the Whites, I have lived With them ever since I was a Boy, and to the best of my Knowledge, I have never Wronged a White Man, on the Contrary, I have always Protected them from the insults of Others, Which they cannot deny. The Four Bears never saw a White Man hungry, but what he gave him to eat. Drink, and a Buffaloe skin to sleep on, in time of Need. I was always ready to die for them, Which they cannot deny. I have done every thing that a red Skin could do for them, and how have they repaid it! With ingratitude! I have Never Called a White Man a Dog, but to day, I do Pronounce them to be a set of Black harted Dogs, they have deceived Me, them that I always considered as Brothers, has turned Out to be My Worst enemies. I have been in Many Battles, and often Wounded, but the Wounds of My enemies I exhalt in, but to day I am Wounded, and by Whom, by those same White Dogs that I have always Considered, and treated as Brothers. I do not fear *Death* my friends. You Know it, but to *die* with my face rotten, that even the Wolves will shrink with horror at seeing Me, and say to themselves, that is the 4 Bears the Friend of the Whites—

Listen well what I have to say, as it will be the last time you will hear Me. think of your Wives, Children, Brothers, Sisters, Friends, and in fact all that you hold dear, are all Dead, or Dying, with their faces all rotten, caused by those dogs the whites, think of all that My friends, and rise all together and Not leave one of them alive.

As you read:
• Do you think Four Bears' change in attitude toward whites was justified? Why or why not?

Four Bears, Second Chief, in Full Dress (1832) by George Catlin.

CORN

AN AMERICAN INDIAN GIFT TO THE WORLD

Early Spanish explorers came to the Americas looking for silver and gold. Their search took them across the two continents, as far north as present-day Kansas and as far south as present-day Peru. Right under their noses, however, were fields planted with a food crop that would enrich the world far greater than gold ever would. Today we call this crop *corn;* American Indians and Europeans called it *maize.*

The Important Discovery of Farming

Between 10,000 and 12,000 years ago, groups of people stopped roaming from place to place in search of food and began to grow crops and raise animals. Exactly how farming began, no one knows for certain. It may have started by

accident when someone dropped seeds into soft, moist soil and discovered that they grew into plants people could eat. For people who took up farming, life changed dramatically. They began to live in communities, and their populations increased rapidly.

The first farmers may have grown crops such as oats or wheat by accidentally planting seeds from wild grasses. Maize, however, never grew wild. Its cultivation was a milestone in farming because it came about through the careful, intentional crossbreeding of different seeds.

Scientists believe that maize was first grown at least 5,000 years ago by ancestors of the Mayas in Central America. Once developed, maize became one of the

Mohawk Indians harvesting corn.

Americas' most important food crops. It proved to be a more dependable food source than game or wild berries. Maize became the mainstay of the Indians of Mexico and Central America. With an abundant food supply, villages and towns that dotted the area grew into cities. From the cities eventually arose the great civilizations of the Olmecs and Toltecs and, later, the Mayas and the Aztecs.

Master Farmers

The American Indians developed farming methods as unique and remarkable as their prize crop. They carefully selected the best corn seeds for planting the next year's crop. They dug holes and planted the seeds rather than simply scattering them on the ground. They developed intricate irrigation systems and cleared away weeds. They learned that maize grew well with beans and squash. The corn plant's broad leaves shaded fragile, young bean and squash plants from the hot sun. The beans used the corn plant's stalk as a stake around which to grow. Squash leaves covered the ground, capturing and conserving moisture, stopping soil erosion, and preventing weed growth. Beans kept the soil rich in nitrogen, which helped the corn and squash grow.

As the empires of the Americas spread, so did maize farming. Traders from Mexico may have introduced maize to other Indian tribes they met, and invading tribes from the north probably learned maize-growing methods.

American Indians developed hundreds of varieties of maize. Different varieties had different flavors and uses. Colors ranged from yellow and red to blue and purple. Some types of maize ripened in sixty days, while others took three or four months to mature.

American Indians also developed numerous ways to prepare and preserve maize. They boiled the ears, ground the kernels into meal, and added water to cornmeal to make dough. They also found many uses for the cobs. Because of their rough surfaces, cobs made fine scrub brushes. Bundled and stood on end, corn cobs served as food graters. Small pieces of cob corked pottery jars. Cobs also provided fuel, and the ashes were sometimes used as medicine.

Maize became so important to many American Indian groups that their religions centered around it. Tribes created their own stories about the origins of maize. Some Indian names for maize translate into English as "Seed of Seed,"

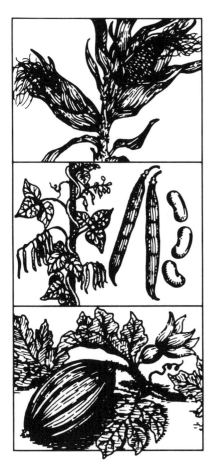

Together, corn, beans, and squash provided a good diet for American Indians.

"Our Mother," and "Our Life." American Indian gods and goddesses represented every part of the plant and the forces that made it grow. Ceremonies and rituals were developed to pay homage to these spirits. The planting and harvesting of maize became important events and were elaborately celebrated. Maize was so much the center of the Mayan culture that the Mayan calendar—one of the world's oldest—was created by farmers to help them keep track of developing maize fields.

When Europeans arrived in 1492, fields of maize grew throughout the Americas. American Indians in the cold climates of Canada and Chile grew rapidly maturing varieties. Inca farmers in Peru planted it on their terraced hillsides in the Andes, and Hopi farmers irrigated extensive maize fields in the dry heat of Arizona and New Mexico. In addition, American Indians cultivated maize along the Missouri and Mississippi rivers and throughout the southeastern region of the United States.

Looking back on the great empires in the Americas, we often think only of their magnificent cities with beautiful temples, pyramids, and floating gardens. Some experts believe the empires would never have been built if the Indians had not developed sophisticated methods of agriculture and a reliable supply of maize to feed their people.

In the Hands of the Europeans
Europeans had no idea what maize was, for the plant did not grow on their continent or in Asia or Africa, where some of them had traveled. Columbus mentioned maize in his log, noting that two of his men had discovered a "sort of grain they called maiz" on the island that is now Cuba. On his return voyage to Spain, Columbus brought back maize.

After its arrival in Europe, maize quickly became a staple crop in Portugal. From there it spread across Europe into southern France and northern Italy. It also spread to Yugoslavia, Romania, Turkey, and China.

Maize fueled population growth in southern Europe during the 1600s and 1700s. People in these regions fed the grain to their animals. Maize helped increase the number of pigs and cattle and improved them as a protein source for humans. A better and more plentiful food supply encouraged Europeans to have larger families.

This Corn Dancer kachina *doll represents a corn spirit worshiped by the Hopi Indians of Arizona. The kachina signifies the importance of corn to the Hopi people.*

Maize in the Americas After 1492

Although Europeans used maize to benefit the people on their own continent, they did not do the same in the Americas for Indians, the first farmers of maize. The conquistadors conquered and enslaved the American Indians, then looted Indian storehouses for grain to feed both themselves and their new slaves. In addition, the Spanish forced the enslaved Indians to help send back to Spain the gold and silver treasures of the once-great Aztec and Inca civilizations.

Later, as other Europeans began to colonize the Americas, they adopted American Indian methods of growing maize. After the Pilgrims landed at Plymouth in present-day Massachusetts in 1620, they had little food. Squanto, an English-speaking Patuxet Indian, taught them how to grow maize. The Pilgrims renamed it *corn*, the name they called any grain they could eat. Soon they were enjoying many American Indian corn foods: hominy, grits, and corn bread. South American colonists ate flat corn breads such as tortillas and tamales.

As more and more European settlers came to the Americas in the 1700s and 1800s, the promise of inexpensive land lured them to North America's Midwest. Farmers in these areas found that when they planted corn, they were assured a harvest. As news of inexpensive, fertile corn land spread, more and more immigrants came to the midwestern United States. They took over lands that were once the homes of many Indian tribes. The area that became known as the Corn Belt extended west from Ohio to Nebraska and Kansas and south to Missouri from Minnesota.

Corn in Africa

Historians believe Turkish traders introduced corn to western Africa. They know that corn was being grown in West Africa by 1550. African farmers welcomed corn and intermixed it with the crops they already grew. Although corn helped many Africans, it played a tragic role in the enslavement of others.

When Europeans first began to colonize the Americas, they often enslaved American Indians to perform the backbreaking labor of developing and working plantations. However, as more and more American Indians died from disease and harsh treatment, plantation owners found themselves with a labor shortage. They believed they could

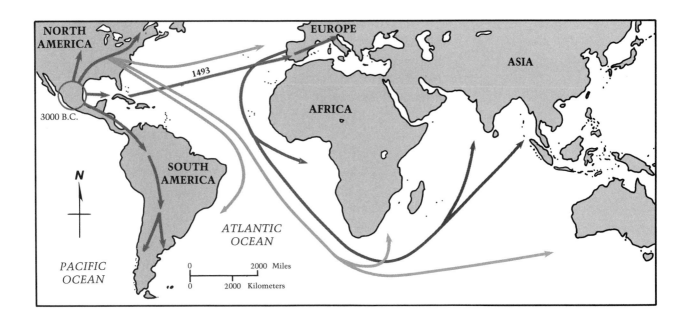

solve their problem by enslaving Africans. The Europeans had developed African trading connections that enabled them to begin slave trade.

The Spread of Corn from the Americas to the Rest of the World

Beginning in the early 1500s, European slave traders from the Caribbean arrived in Africa. The slavers traded guns, cloth, and tools for Africans who had been kidnapped and enslaved by rival tribes. On the slave ships, slaves were packed tightly together, chained back to back, and kept alive by a diet of beans and corn meal. Under these conditions, they made the two- to four-month journey to the islands of the Caribbean.

In this way, corn, which had great life-giving potential for people in Africa, contributed to the enslavement of millions of Africans. As the slave trade continued, corn was planted near the African slave ports so that a plentiful supply was always readily available to feed enslaved Africans on the voyages to the Americas.

Corn Today and Tomorrow

Today, corn is one of the world's four basic food grains. Because it can grow in so many climates and soils, more than 300 million acres of land worldwide are planted with corn. Farmers grow more than fifteen billion bushels of corn every year.

Most of us enjoy eating corn and food made from corn

such as breakfast cereals, tortillas, salad dressings, marshmallows, ice cream, and margarine. In the United States, we eat only about one of seven bushels of corn grown. Much of the remainder feeds farm livestock. Part of our corn crop is used in ways never imagined by its first farmers. Over 1,000 items are made from corn or corn by-products, including cardboard, crayons, lubricants, plastics, wallpaper, antibiotics, rayon, deodorants, mouthwash, soap, and packaging material!

A recent development that holds great promise for the future is the use of corn to make fuel for cars and trucks. Corn is processed into a fuel called *ethanol,* which can be used by itself or blended with gasoline. Ethanol burns very cleanly and does not emit as much pollution into the air as gasoline. Also, ethanol can be produced on a regular, ongoing basis, because corn can be grown annually. Experts believe ethanol can help reduce our need for oil, a resource that cannot be renewed.

For thousands of years, American Indians respected the value of corn. As expert farmers, Indians learned how to breed corn that would grow in many different climates. Only 500 years ago this simple food grain began its worldwide journey from the shores of the Americas. Today people all over the world share in this American Indian gift.

A Better Packaging Alternative

Many companies currently use plastic foam pellets or paper to fill voids and protect the contents in boxes packed for shipping. Paper is heavy and expensive, and its manufacture requires the cutting of trees. Plastic foam does not decompose easily. In some cases plastic foam can take several hundred years to decompose. Also, the foam adds to limited landfill space when it is thrown away.

The corn industry is experimenting with a new lightweight packing material made from corn starch. The corn starch pellets add little weight to the packing box. Even better, the pellets are made from a resource that can be renewed annually, and they decompose in water.

One kind of corn starch packing material.

THANK THE AMERICAN INDIAN

Herbert J. Spinden

When Herbert J. Spinden wrote "Thank the American Indian," in 1928, he was Curator of Mexican Archeology and Ethnology at the Peabody Museum at Harvard University. Throughout the 1920s, the United States experienced good food-crop growing conditions. In this essay, Spinden examines the separate but parallel development of cultures of the Old World (Africa, Asia, and Europe) and the New World (North and South America). He explores the significance of American food plants as they spread from the Americas throughout the world.

The present [1928] economic position of the United States, the strongest of any country on earth, is due in a large measure to the plants, materials, and processes which constitute our inheritance from the ancient civilizations of American Indians. Well over half of our total agricultural wealth, in fact about four sevenths of it, consists of crops unknown in the Old World until after the momentous voyage of Columbus.

The value of this Indian inheritance annually reaches sums beyond the dreams of avarice [greed]. Farm values amount to billions of dollars and other billions of dollars are developed in the commercial turnover. But, indeed, the entire world is benefited by gifts from Indian farmers and the indications are that the economic importance of the ancient products of the New World civilization will increase rather than diminish in the future.

Man came into America from Asia on the Neolithic [latest period of the Stone Age] plane of life, bringing bows and arrows, stone axes and knives, but having no metals and no food supply in the form of domesticated plants and animals. The tribes who remained behind in the Old World and those who immigrated to America started, as it were, from scratch in a race for the higher honors of civilization. At the time of the separation,

As you read:
- **Why does any civilization need a reliable food supply?**
- **What does a reliable food supply allow a civilization to accomplish?**

neither group had found a stable food supply. But afterwards, each group managed to do so with the materials at hand, entirely ignorant of what was being done by other human beings with other materials, half the world around.

Yet the results obtained by completely independent means are remarkably parallel. Higher achievements of social life depended directly upon ample food supply; the exact nature of this food supply was relatively unimportant so long as a balanced diet was reached. Ample food supply allowed population to multiply, and specialization in industry to take place. Kings, priests and artists were independently evolved by society in the two severed hemispheres.

In such an art as architecture, similar methods of construction and decoration were invented. The Mayas, for example, learned how to lay beautiful courses of cut stone, to make lime mortar [a cement-like building material] from limestone by burning, to handle stucco [plaster] decorations and fresco painting [painting on moist plaster] on temple walls. Their use of mortar and rubble [rough broken stones] for walls and ceilings gives a modern touch to the picture, as does their fondness for skyscraper effects. They even discovered how to burn bricks as a substitute for stone, as is seen clearly enough at the early city of Comalcalco. Similarly in weaving, the parts of the loom were independently invented in America; and in metal work, gilding, plating and casting by the lost wax processes [a type of metal casting] were discovered.

Under all this Indian culture, and making it possible, were plants furnishing food, fiber and other substances which had been tamed to the garden. We are accustomed to judge the excellence of dead civilization by works of art but perhaps a fairer judgment might be based on the way the primary problems of living were solved and the gregarious [social] instinct given a chance to produce social organizations.

The nuclear [central] civilization of the New World came into being on the highlands of Mexico and Central America as a result of the domestication of maize, beans, and squashes. Agriculture made possible the culture which we now call "archaic" and which must have begun several thousand years before the birth of Christ. The art of this archaic civilization of the first American farmers has mostly passed away, excepting pottery objects. Most interesting of these are figurines of men and women. The archaic civilization spread north and south through arid lands and the spread of plants was accompanied by the spread of weaving and pottery making.

Then came the great burst of the Mayan supremacy, due to economic conquest of the humid tropics, beginning about 1000 B.C. The old series of plants were modified to meet wet land conditions and new plants were domesticated that were indigenous [native] to the wet land. The Mayas themselves were the first to domesticate cacao, which Linnaeus [a Swedish botanist] afterwards named *Theobroma*, food of the gods. Chocolate is made from the prepared seeds of this domesticated tree. Cacao pods attached to the tree trunk in characteristic fashion are unmistakably represented in several sculptures at Copan, dating from the Fifth Century A.D. The Mayas also tamed the fruits called papaya, zapote, anona, alligator pear, and so on, and discovered the virtues of vanilla as a flavoring substance. Also to the Mexican and Central American field we must ascribe tomatoes and peppers in wide variety.

The idea of agriculture took root in North and South America as a result of the actual spread of maize, beans, and squashes, but local plants were also brought under cultivation in several regions. For North America, outside of Mexico, the list of indigenous food plants is small: the principal items being Jerusalem artichokes and the strawberries which Captain John Smith found under cultivation in Virginia. But sugar was drawn from the sap of several species of maple by the woodland Indians, while blueberries and cranberries would doubtless have been domesticated except for their natural profusion.

In South America the indigenous food plants include the potato of the Andes, while in the rich Amazon valley a number of valuable foods including manioc, the sweet potato, the peanut, the pineapple and so on, were brought under cultivation. Most of these seem to have been domesticated by the Arawaks in Brazil but the area of their pre-Columbian distribution included Central America and the West Indies. There are numerous minor foods in tropical America which need not be listed.

Indian farmers did their job well and succeeded in establishing many useful differentiations in their food plants. Indeed the original set of plants, namely maize, beans and squashes, were carried very far from wild types and given wider range in climactic adaptation than any comparable plants of Old World origin. Maize grows from Canada to Argentina in arid and humid lands and at high and low elevations. Squashes and

Pottery of a Mayan earth god emerging from a corn stalk.

pumpkins are tremendously differentiated yet there are believed to be only two basic species. Also there are two basic species of the legumes we now call beans, namely the *Phaseolus vulgaris* and the *Phaseolus lunatus,* but out of these come more varieties than can be mustered by the peas and lentils of the Old World. The Mandan Indians of North Dakota, on the margin of agriculture, had corn that would mature in 60 days and they also had rapidly maturing squashes and several distinct varieties of beans. . . .

Maize was introduced into the Old World shortly after the discovery of America. It was favorably received by the Turks and from them it passed eastward across Asia, reaching China about 1540. It must be remembered that at this time the Turks were a wide-awake dominant people and that caravan trade to the Far East was largely in their hands. Maize is often called Turkey grain in Europe and it is of some interest that two American birds, the turkey and the muscovy duck are given European names from the European regions of first acceptance. Also the Turks took to tobacco [originally grown by American Indians] from the first and now have varieties in their own name. Another case of adoption is the potato which is now called Irish simply because it lifted an Irish famine.

In Chinese archives the references to the introduction of maize are explicit. Instructions were given that the yield be turned in as taxes in order that the government could distribute seed. Today [1928] maize is an important food in Italy and the Balkans. It thrives in South Africa and in parts of Australia. It is the most valuable single crop in the United States. . . .

In the Old World, the emphasis was on domesticated animals, but this source is so uneconomical that the use of flesh will doubtless decrease in the future. On the other hand, American Indian plants such as maize, potatoes and sweet potatoes head the list as giving the greatest yields of human food for a given acreage in temperate [having a mild climate] lands, maize being nearly twice as serviceable as wheat in this regard. There is good reason to believe, then, that the foods of the American Indian will be increasingly important to all humanity and that the arts and other social achievements of the New World will gain prestige as time rolls on.

HISTORY OF
THE NEW WORLD

Giralamo Benzoni

*Historians think Columbus introduced maize to Europe on the
return trip from his first voyage in 1493. From Portugal and
Spain, maize spread across southern Europe and on to Turkey
in Asia. Italian historian Giralamo Benzoni, who was
probably familiar with maize in Europe, traveled in the
Americas from 1541 to 1556. He most likely saw maize growing nearly everywhere. In the following excerpt from his book,*
History of the New World, *Benzoni gives a detailed description
of American Indian preparation of food from maize.*

The grain of these people [in southern Mexico] is commonly
called *maize,* and came from *La Española,* which island was
first discovered by the Christians; wine is *chichia;* their boats,
canoue; swords are *macanne;* their chiefs are *caciques.* They do
not prepare the earth for sowing their grain, but making a small
hole they put in three or four grains, and covering it over suf-
fices; each stem produces three or four ears, containing about a
hundred grains each. The stems of the maize are taller than a
man, and in some provinces they harvest twice a year.

The women, *molandaie,* who grind it, wet a quantity of this
grain the previous evening with cold water, and in the morning
they gradually triturate [grind] it between two stones. Some
stand up to it, others kneel on the ground; nor do they care if
any hairs fall into it, or even some *pidocchi* [lice]. When they
have made a mass by sprinkling in water with the hand, they
shape it into little loaves, either long or round, and putting
them into some leaves of reeds, with as little water as possible,
they cook them. This is the common people's bread; it lasts
two days and then mildews. The chief's bread is made in the
following way: after soaking and triturating the corn between
two stones, the *molandaie* wash it with hot water and pick out
the husk, leaving only the flour, which they grind as much as

A woman in the southwest-
ern United States grinding
corn into flour.

they can and then shape it into small cakes. These are cooked
in a round pipkin [small pot], applying fire under them by
degrees. There is great trouble in making this bread, and it is
not good but when fresh, and not very good then nor when
cold; indeed, maize is not good either hot or cold. Travelling in
uninhabited districts, and with necessity for my guide, I
learned to grind it, in order not to eat it raw or roasted. On
account of its great hardness the grinding is very severe work,
and when I had but little maize I did not pick out the husks as
the chief's people do; nor did grinding it fine suit my arms, that
were very thin and weak.

MAIZE

Garcilaso de la Vega

Garcilaso de la Vega (1539–1616) was born in Cuzco, the ancient capital of the Incas in Peru. His father was a Spanish conquistador of noble birth; his mother is said to have been a princess descended from Inca emperors. In 1560 de la Vega left Peru for Spain to claim the honors due his father. When he learned of the Spanish attempt to destroy and discredit the Inca civilization, he wrote Royal Commentaries of the Incas and General History of Peru, *a history of Inca grandeur. In this excerpt, de la Vega describes Inca foods made from maize and reveals the importance of corn to the Incas.*

The fruits of the earth on which the natives of Peru lived before the Spaniards came were of various kinds, some of which grew above ground and others below it. Of the fruits that grew above ground the most important was the grain the Mexicans and the inhabitants of the Windward Islands call maize and the Peruvians *sara,* for it is their bread. It is of two kinds, one hard kind called *murchu,* the other soft and very tasty, called *capia.* They eat it instead of bread, roasted or boiled in plain water. The seed of the hard maize is the kind that has been introduced into Spain: the soft sort has not been brought here [Spain]. In some provinces it is softer and tenderer than in others, especially in the province called Rucana. For their solemn sacrifices, they used . . . a maize loaf called *çancu,* and they made the same bread to eat as an occasional delicacy; they called it *huminta.* The two names were applied, not because the bread was any different, but because one kind was used for sacrifices and the other simply for eating. The flour was ground by the women on broad flat stones. They laid the grain on one of these and applied to it another stone, shaped like a rather elongated half moon, though not rounded. It would be about three fingers broad, and the women held it by the two points of the half-moon and moved it to and fro on the maize. In this clumsy way they ground their corn and anything else they needed to grind: because of the difficulty of the process they did not eat bread regularly.

They did not grind with pestle [a club-shaped tool for grinding] and mortar [a vessel in which material is ground], though they had these implements. Grinding in a mortar is done by the force of blows, but the moon-shaped stone grinds whatever comes under it by its own weight and the Indian women can easily handle it because of its shape, rocking it to and fro and occasionally heaping the grounds in the middle of the flat stone with one hand so as to grind them over again, while the other hand is left free to hold the grindstone, which we might reasonably describe as a *batán* [mill] from the strokes given alternately by the two hands. This method of grinding is still in use. They also made porridge, which they call *api*, and ate it with great relish, because it was only consumed on rare occasions.

To complete our account, the flour was separated from the bran by pouring it on to a clean cotton cloth and smoothing it over with the hand. The pure flour is so fine that it sticks to the cloth while the bran, being coarser, remains detached and is easily removed. The fine flour is collected in the middle of the cloth and poured out; then more is put on the cloth until the necessary quantity has been sifted. The sifting of flour was intended for the bread consumed by the Spaniards rather than for Indian use, since the latter were not so particular as to turn up their noses at bran, and the bran is not so rough, especially that from soft maize, as to need to be removed. The sifting was done in the fashion we have described for want of sieves [sifting devices], which only arrived from Spain with the introduction of wheat. I have seen all this with my own eyes, and until I was nine or ten years old I was brought up on *sara* or *maize*. . . .

With maize flour the Spaniards make little biscuits, fritters, and other dainties for invalids and the healthy. As a remedy in all sorts of treatment experienced doctors have rejected wheat flour in favor of maize flour. The same flour is mixed with plain water to brew their beverage, which can be soured in the Indian fashion to make a very good vinegar. An excellent honey is made from the unripe cane, which is very sweet. The dried canes and their leaves are of great value, and cattle are very fond of them. The leaves from the ear of maize and the stalks are used by those who make statues who thus avoid weight. Some Indians, who are more intent on getting drunk than the rest, place the *sara* in steep [liquid] and keep it there until it

Inca poster showing corn harvesting.

SEEDS • OF • CHANGE

begins to sprout. They then grind it and boil it in the same water as other things. Once this is strained it is kept until it ferments. A very strong drink, which intoxicates immediately, is thus produced. It is called *viñapu,* or in another language *sora.* The Incas forbade its use since it at once produces drunkenness, but I am told that it has recently been revived by some vicious people. Thus the advantages I have mentioned are all derived from the various parts of the *sora,* and there are many other medical derivatives, both beverages and plasters [bandage-like coverings], as we shall have occasion to mention later.

The second most important of the crops that are grown above ground is that called *quinua,* or in Spanish "millet" or "little rice" which it rather resembles in the color and appearance of the grain. The plant is rather like the wild amaranth in stalk, leaf, and flower: it is the latter that produces the *quinua.* The Indians eat the tender leaves in cooked dishes, for they are very tasty and nourishing. They eat the grain in pottages [thick soups] prepared in many different ways. The Indians also brew a drink from the *quinua,* as they do from maize, but it is only produced in regions where maize does not grow. The Indian inhabitants use flour made of *quinua* in various illnesses. In 1590 I was sent some of the seeds from Peru, but they were dead, and though planted at different times never sprouted.

In addition, the Peruvian Indians have three or four kinds of beans, shaped like broad beans but smaller: they are quite good to eat, and are used in cooked dishes. They are called *purutu.* They have lupins [beanlike seeds] like those in Spain, though rather larger and whiter: they are called *tarui.* Apart from the edible types, there are others not suitable for eating: they are round and look like cut turquoises, though they have many different colors and are about as big as chick-peas. The general word for them is *chuy,* but they are given various names according to the color. Some of these names are comic and others are appropriate, but we shall not include them so as to avoid prolixity [wordiness]. They are used in many different games played by boys and by grown men: I remember taking part in both sorts.

THE STRANGE ORIGIN OF CORN

Abnaki

American Indians expressed spiritual beliefs through paintings, carvings, dances, and storytelling. Their legends were about the beauty of the landscape, the customs of a tribe, and the origins of plants or animals. The legend that follows is from the Abnaki tribe of present-day Maine. The introduction to the legend in the paragraph that follows was written by Margot Edmonds and Ella E. Clark, authors of a book of Indian legends entitled Voices of the Winds.

The main body of Abnaki was in western Maine, mostly in the valleys of the Dennebec, Androscoggin, and Sacos rivers, and the neighboring coast. They originally emigrated from the Southwest [in the United States], having encountered John Cabot [a British-paid explorer] in 1498; but the Indians had no other dealings with white people at that time. In 1604, Champlain [a French explorer] passed along the coast and visited Abnaki bands. In 1607 and 1608 the Plymouth Company [in Massachusetts] made an unsuccessful effort to form a permanent settlement at the mouth of the Kennebec. Later, the Abnaki withdrew to Canada, settling around St. Francis [in the province of Quebec].

A long time ago, when the Indians were first made, one man lived alone, far from any others. He did not know fire, and so he lived on roots, bark, and nuts. This man became very lonely for companionship. He grew tired of digging roots, lost his appetite, and for several days lay dreaming in the sunshine. When he awoke, he saw someone standing near and, at first, was very frightened.

But when he heard the stranger's voice, his heart was glad, and he looked up. He saw a beautiful woman with long *light* hair! "Come to me," he whispered. But she did not, and when he tried to approach her she moved farther away. He sang to her about his loneliness, and begged her not to leave him.

At last she replied, "If you will do exactly what I tell you to do, I will also be with you."

He promised that he would try his very best. So she led him to a place where there was some very dry grass. "Now get two dry sticks," she told him, "and rub them together fast while you hold them in the grass."

Soon a spark flew out. The grass caught fire, and as swiftly as an arrow takes flight, the ground was burned over. Then the beautiful woman spoke again: "When the sun sets, take me by the hair and drag me over the burned ground."

"Oh, I don't want to do that!" the man exclaimed.

"You must do what I tell you to do," said she. "Wherever you drag me, something like grass will spring up, and you will see something like hair coming from between the leaves. Soon seeds will be ready for your use."

The man followed the beautiful woman's orders. And when the Indians see silk on the cornstalk, they know that the beautiful woman has not forgotten them.

The earliest known picture of maize to appear in Europe. The picture, published in a botany book in 1542, aroused great interest in the new crop.

MILLIONS IN TASSEL

Dorothy Giles

In 1940, Dorothy Giles traced the history of corn in her book Singing Valleys: The Story of Corn. *Extensive corn farming by European immigrants spread from the northeastern United States down the Ohio River Valley. In the early 1800s land along the Mississippi River became available at low prices. Immigrants worked hard to save money to begin corn farming. In the following excerpt, Giles captures the spirit of early corn farming in the American Midwest.*

As you read:
- **How did the dreams of immigrant farmers clash with the traditional use of the land by American Indians?**
- **Did Indians have a right to the land? Explain your views.**

In Cleveland, in Chicago, in Detroit, the foreigners [immigrants] found work. Any work did, so long as it allowed them to save toward the purchase of land. . . .

As soon as they had a yoke of oxen, a home-made wagon, tools, a plow, sacks of corn, they left the towns and started out across the prairie. The matted grass was hard to break; but a swing of an axe, and there would be a deep gash into which to drop four kernels of corn. . . . They tamped the earth down over the seed with their heavy boots, and moved on two steps to swing and axe again. And again.

The roots of the corn did what their tools would not do. They broke the tenacious prairie sod. Next year it was possible to put a plowshare into the ground and to drive a long straight furrow. The earth that rippled away from the blade was dark and rich and sweet to smell.

Soon there were a sod hut and a cornfield where there had been only prairie grass. Some day there would be a cluster of farm buildings, a silo, a mill. Then a village with a school and a church. Years later there was a railroad station and a post office. And after that, many houses, gas-filling stations, a movie theatre, Coca-Cola signs in Neon lights, beauty shoppes—a city. . . .

The years 1835 to 1836 marked the heyday of speculation in government lands, even though ten years later Wisconsin was offering 500,000 acres at $1.25 per acre on thirty years' credit. The interest of seven percent was collectable annually in

Farmers planting corn in the United States during the 1870s.

advance. A man with one hundred dollars in cash who went into that country moved like a prince. Speculators were quick to take advantage of the bargain and bought vast tracts which they held, and then resold at double the government's price.

Meanwhile, in Chicago, in Kansas City, in Minneapolis, the corn from the farms was sold either in its natural state as grain, or as hogs and lard. Not only the men who raised these but men who traded in them in the cities grew rich.

A Peace Chief Speaks

Shabonee, a chief of the midwestern Potawatomi tribe, favored peace with the white settlers. Speaking in 1827, he gives his views on the futility of war with the settlers.

In my youthful days, I have seen large herds of buffalo on these prairies, and elk were found in every grove, but they are here no more, having gone towards the setting sun. For hundreds of miles no white man lived, but now trading posts and settlers are found here and there throughout the country, and in a few years the smoke from their cabins will be seen to ascend from every grove, and the prairie covered with their cornfields. . . .

The red man must leave the land of his youth and find a new home in the far west. The armies of the whites are without number, like the sands of the sea, and ruin will follow all tribes that go to war with them.

THE
POTATO
ANDEAN FOOD
FOR
MILLIONS

$\mathbf{F}$rom terraced Andean mountainsides in South America came the lumpy and not-so-pretty potato, a plant that, like corn, would feed millions around the world. Many nutritional experts consider the potato an almost-perfect food. It provides a good combination of vitamins, minerals, and fiber. Eaten by itself, the potato has no fat and almost no sodium. Some nutritionists believe a diet of whole milk and potatoes can supply practically all the nourishment humans need for good health.

The potato is a vegetable. It is a *tuber,* or storage stem. The tuber grows underground, providing food to the plant's leafy stems and white flowers above ground. The tuber is the only part of the potato plant that can be eaten.

Scientists believe the potato first grew wild around Lake Titicaca in the central part of the Andes Mountains, between Peru and western Bolivia. At 12,507 feet elevation, Titicaca is the world's highest lake. More than 7,000 years ago, the people who roamed through the Andes collected wild potatoes. Over hundreds of years they developed methods for growing them.

The Incas and the Potato

At the time of Columbus's first voyage, Incas living in the Andes Mountains were producing more than 3,000 kinds of potatoes. The geography of the Andes and the intelligence and hard work of the Incas made such a variety

Incas digging potatoes. The poster is one of a series based on the Incan calendar.

of potatoes possible. The Andes lie along the Pacific Ocean side of South America. This craggy mountain range—the world's longest—stretches north to south for nearly 4,500 miles from Panama to the southern tip of Chile. The Inca empire was spread along 2,000 miles of this mountainous terrain, from present-day Colombia to Argentina.

Scientists think the Incas first settled in the Andes Mountains around Lake Titicaca about 1,500 years ago. To cultivate potatoes, the Incas leveled small areas up and down the mountainsides into flattened fields called *terraces*. They constructed canals to carry water from one field to another to irrigate the crops. This multilevel farming method meant that each terrace had its own type of soil, growing climate, and moisture condition. The length of the growing season varied with the altitude.

The Andes climate ranges from very warm in the subtropic and tropical regions to very cold in the southern regions near the Antarctic. Mountainside farming allowed the Incas to experiment and develop different kinds of potatoes for different climate zones. The Incas produced potatoes of all sizes, textures, and colors, from whites and yellows to browns, purples, oranges, and reds. Some types of potatoes were sweet and suitable for humans to eat. Some were too bitter for human taste, but good for livestock feed. Some kinds matured quickly, some slowly. Some varieties required a lot of water, some very little.

The First Dried Potatoes

Inca experimentation with the potato extended to methods of storage, as well. In fact, the Incas invented the first "freeze-dried" potatoes. To preserve potatoes, the Incas made them into *chuño*, a dried potato product. Spreading the potatoes on the ground, the Incas left them overnight to freeze. The next day they walked on the potatoes to squeeze out the water, then left them to dry in the sun. This process was repeated for four or five days until the potatoes were thoroughly dry. As chuño, the potatoes could be stored for several years, then reconstituted by adding water.

The Incas' farming methods allowed them to grow corn and beans as well as potatoes. Producing a variety of crops helped ensure against food shortages. If one crop failed, another was likely to survive and provide enough food for the population. The potato, however, was the Incas' most

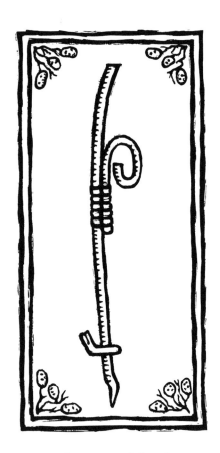

Incan digging tool for planting and harvesting potatoes.

important crop and helped the civilization grow into a huge empire. The Incas clearly understood the importance of the potato to their empire. Inca art forms used images of the vegetable, and the people worshiped potato spirits in their religious ceremonies.

The Potato Spreads to Europe

The potato did not immediately attract the attention of the conquering Spanish. When Spanish conquistadors arrived to conquer Peru in 1531, they were mostly interested in the Incas' gold and silver. To mine the precious metals, the conquistadors enslaved the Incas and fed them chuño from Inca storehouses.

It is not known exactly when and how the potato traveled from Peru to Europe and back to North America. Historians do know that the conquistadors fed potatoes to the sailors on Spanish ships. The Spanish sailors probably took the potato from South America or the Caribbean islands to Europe, especially Spain.

The potato was not an immediate hit in Europe. Europeans rejected it for several reasons. For one thing, they did not usually eat root crops. They preferred grains that could be milled and baked or cooked in a porridge, such as oatmeal or gruel. Some people believed eating potatoes would be a sin because potatoes were not mentioned in the Bible. Agriculturalists in France declared potatoes would destroy the soil. Some medical experts of the time believed the potato would cause leprosy and other diseases because it was such an ugly, misshapen plant.

Although some farmers in northern Spain began to grow potatoes around 1600, the vegetable remained little more than a curiosity for almost two centuries. Monks grew it in monastery gardens, and the wealthy upper classes ate it as a novelty food. European peasants continued to ignore it until late in the 1700s. Even then, peasants in many countries planted the crop only because their rulers forced them to.

Once planted, however, potatoes took root not only in European soil, but in European daily life. Peasants quickly discovered that a field of potatoes produced more nutritious food than that same field planted in any grain. Potatoes matured in three or four months, a much shorter time than that of many grains, and could grow in a variety of soils. Potatoes cultivation required much less attention than

The potato "eye" design on this ancient Peruvian pot shows the importance of potatoes.

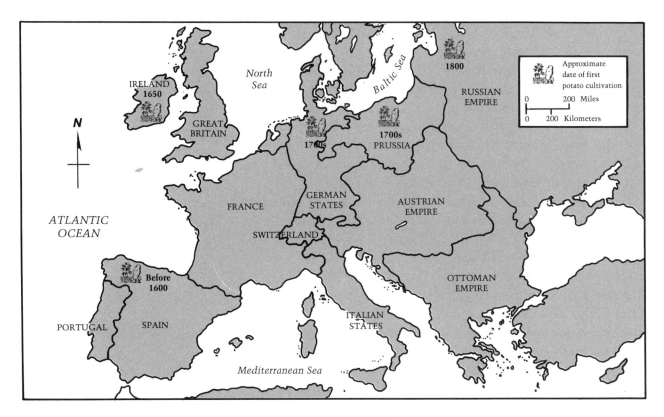

The Spread of the Potato in Europe. *Each date indicates the approximate year in which potatoes were first grown in the country indicated.*

grain, and far fewer workers were needed to harvest the crop. Because the edible portion of the potato grew underground, it could not be damaged or destroyed by wind, hail, heavy rains, snow, birds, or most animals.

The Potato Changes Europe

Perhaps the potato's most important contribution was its fueling of Europe's Industrial Revolution during the 1700s and 1800s. During these centuries, great changes happened because of *industrialization,* the process of using machines to do work previously done by people.

Before the potato was brought to Europe, almost all Europeans were farmers. Most grew only the amount of food their families needed to survive. One potato plant, however, produced three or more potatoes. A field of potato plants produced many more potatoes than one family could eat. By planting potatoes, farmers could feed their families and have some left over to sell.

With a steady supply of food available for purchase, many farmers moved to cities and became factory workers, running machines to make cloth, clothing, farm tools, and many other products. With the money they earned in facto-

SEEDS · OF · CHANGE

ries, workers bought the foods they needed from farmers—including nutritious potatoes.

Industrialization changed Europe from a continent of small farms and villages to a continent of manufacturing cities. Without a reliable supply of inexpensive, nutritious potatoes, Europe's industrialization would certainly have taken much longer.

Ireland: When the Potato Failed

Nowhere in Europe did the potato become more important than in Ireland, the small island country west of England. Between 1649 and 1652, the English, under Oliver Cromwell, conquered Ireland, driving thousands of people from their homes and into the westernmost part of the country. This area had very poor soil and too much rain for growing grains. The refugees faced starvation.

During the same period, Spanish fishermen who dried their catches on Ireland's western beaches introduced potatoes to the hungry Irish. Eager for a reliable crop, the Irish soon learned how to grow potato plants. They discovered that the number of potatoes produced on just one acre of land could feed a family for a year. During the next 200 years, Irish farmers stopped growing almost all other crops and planted mostly potatoes. The adoption of the potato was so successful in Ireland that the vegetable supported a population explosion. In 1760, Ireland had one and a half million people. By 1840, only eighty years later, the country had nine million people .

Unfortunately, the dependence on the potato had devastating consequences for the Irish in 1845–1846, when potato blight, a plant-killing disease, spread rapidly through the countryside, striking crop after crop. Potatoes rotted and died in the ground. During the blight, more than 750,000 Irish people died of starvation or disease. Others were evicted from their homes and tiny plots of land when they could not pay rent to their landlords because of failed crops.

To escape death, thousands of Irish came to the United States by ship. Many of them made their homes in east coast cities such as New York and Boston. Irish men often took jobs building railroads and digging canals. Some Irish women worked in sewing rooms making shirts and dresses. The Irish migration continued for years, increasing the population of the United States and decreasing that of Ireland.

The Potato Today and Tomorrow

The story of the potato did not end with massive European emigration to the United States. Today, the potato is rooted in the agriculture and diet of most of the world's countries. China today harvests more than twice as many potatoes as all the countries of North America from Panama through Canada. The story of how the potato spread is not yet over. Scientists are developing potato seeds that will make potato planting easier and will increase production. They are hoping that new kinds of potatoes will help feed people in African and Asian countries who face the constant threat of starvation.

Five hundred years ago, Columbus and later the Spanish conquistadors came to the Americas in search of gold and silver. Perhaps the conquistadors should have paid more attention to the humble potato. Today, one year's worldwide potato crop is worth more money than all the gold the Spanish took from the Americas.

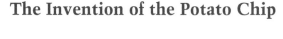

The Invention of the Potato Chip

Potato chips are one of America's favorite snack foods. The average American eats about four pounds of potato chips per year.

The world's first potato chips were created by an American Indian, George Crum. One day in 1853, a diner at the Moon Lake Lodge resort in Saratoga Springs, New York, returned his French fries, saying they were too thick and too soggy. Mr. Crum, the lodge chef, sliced the potatoes very thin and fried them in oil for about thirty minutes. After removing them from the oil, he salted them heavily.

The customer was delighted. Crum's "Saratoga Chips" became a house specialty. Soon people in many parts of the country were making potato chips.

AMERICAN FOOD CROPS IN THE OLD WORLD

William H. McNeill

William H. McNeill is a prominent American historian with a special interest in the history of the potato. His analysis here is on the impact of the potato in Ireland and throughout Europe. The excerpt is part of a chapter from the book Seeds of Change, *published by the Smithsonian Institution Press.*

The potato was native to the altiplano [high plateau or plain] of Peru, where it provided the principal food for the Incas and their subject populations. Shortly after the Spaniards conquered Peru in 1536, Spanish ships operating in Pacific waters off the coast of Peru and Chile began to use potatoes as a cheap food for sailors. But since men and goods going to Spain usually crossed the isthmus of Panama by caravan, so bulky a food as potatoes got left behind. But once in a while, when a ship left the Pacific and headed for home around the Horn or through the treacherous Strait of Magellan its store of potatoes might last all the way to Spain.

In this entirely unrecorded fashion, the new food eventually reached the Old World. Before the end of the sixteenth century Basque sailors' families along the Biscay coast of northern Spain became the earliest European population to make room in their gardens for the new crop. They used it as it had been used along the Pacific coast of South America, as shipboard food. Fishermen, operating off the coast of Ireland from northern Spanish ports, before 1650 transmitted potatoes to the Irish, who then established an entirely new style of subsistence farming on the basis of potatoes alone.

Once potatoes came ashore in Europe, learned botanists, interested in novelties from the Americas, discovered the recent import (again in unrecorded ways). It entered the literary record for the first time when John Gerard published his *Herball, or generall historie of plantes* in 1597. Gerard took special pride in his discovery and used a woodcut of a flowering potato plant as the frontispiece [illustration preceding the title page] of his book. He praised the food value of the tubers. . . .

The literary record tells us nothing about how potatoes spread to the gardens of ordinary people from the original lodgment along the coast of northern Spain. Spread they did, but, except in Ireland, they remained a relatively unimportant garden vegetable until peasant cultivators saw how useful it would be to have more potatoes on hand when military requisitioning threatened their grain stocks. This happened first in what is now Belgium, when Louis XIV's wars ravaged the land in the 1680s. Potatoes then spread across Germany and Poland in the eighteenth century, becoming important in southwestern Germany during the War of the Spanish Succession (1700–1713) and reaching eastward into Prussia and Poland during the Seven Years' War (1756–63). The Revolutionary and Napoleonic Wars (1792–1815) brought the potato to Russia and intensified its cultivation throughout the whole north European plain. Indeed, potato acreage increased during every subsequent European war, including World War II. That was because, given the soil and climate of northern Europe, no other crop produces as many calories per acre; and when food gets short, extra calories become irresistible.

The advantage was counterbalanced by a difficulty. Potatoes do not last in storage nearly as well as grain. Carryover from one year to the next is impossible, since stored potatoes start to sprout and then to rot. As a result, a population depending wholly on potatoes risks real disaster in case of crop failure. That is what happened to the Irish in 1845–46 when a fungus arrived from America (on fast, new steamships) and destroyed the fields of potatoes upon which they had become dependent.

Ireland was, indeed, the first European land in which potatoes became really important. As elsewhere, war triggered the shift to the new crop. Between 1649 and 1652, Cromwell's Roundheads* conquered the whole of Ireland, and his government decided to make the island safe for English Protestantism by settling army veterans on Irish soil, while confining the native Irish to the westernmost province of Connacht. This

This French illustration from the 1600s shows a farmer paying his taxes— farm products—to a tax collector.

———————

*Roundheads, so-called because of their short haircuts, were followers of Oliver Cromwell. Because the Irish had sided with the opposition in the English Civil War, Cromwell conquered Ireland.

SEEDS • OF • CHANGE

created a severe crisis for the thousands of Irishmen who were uprooted from their homes and driven into the rain-soaked western part of the island. Grain could not ripen there, and pastureland was insufficient to support the refugees. Survivors found a solution by cultivating potatoes, brought ashore by Basque fishermen at places where they were accustomed to drying their catch before returning home.

Once the Irish learned how to cultivate the new plant, and discovered that a whole family could live on a single acre of potato land, they were able to undercut the army veterans that Cromwell's government had planted in other provinces of Ireland. The Irish could afford to work for English landlords (who remained in possession of most of Ireland until the twentieth century) by offering their labor at much cheaper rates than Englishmen, who insisted on eating bread, were willing to do. Ireland was thus restored to the Irish in the course of the eighteenth and early nineteenth centuries, but only at the cost of abject poverty and an almost total dependence on a diet of potatoes.

Ireland in fact developed a two-tiered society and economy. Landlords hired Irish laborers to produce beef and other commodities for sale, usually in England. But for most of the population, wages only slightly modified a subsistence economy; rural laborers simply channeled their income into the rent for a bit of land on which they planted the potatoes they needed to feed themselves. When blight struck in 1845–46, the great majority of the Irish had absolutely no reserve of food. Hundreds of thousands died before public relief could be organized. Other scores of thousands emigrated to America and elsewhere beyond the seas. Back home, survivors began a slow, angry climb back towards political sovereignty and the mixed farming that prevails today, in which cattle, hogs, and horses matter more than potatoes.

On the Continent and in England, potatoes never displaced grain growing and mixed farming. Accordingly, the blight of 1845–46 did not create outright famine, as in Ireland, although failure of the potato crop did create (or at least exacerbate) the food shortages of the "Hungry Forties," which were long remembered by Europe's poorer classes. In 1847, drier summer weather checked the blight, and eventually sprays and blight-resistant varieties forestalled repetition of the massive crop failures of 1845–46.

Impoverished Irish women in their sod hut.

As population mounted in Germany and elsewhere across the north European plain, potatoes ceased to be only a fallow [unused] field crop. With other new crops like sugar beets, they began to encroach on rye fields, and the poorer classes began to eat more and more potatoes and less and less bread. But outright dependence on a single food that had characterized the Irish before 1845 never arose on the European continent. Even the poorest German, Polish, and Russian farmers were able to supplement their diet of potatoes with other foods—especially cabbages, beets, and bread. Nevertheless, throughout northern Europe, potatoes dominated the diet of the poor in the nineteenth and twentieth centuries. This in turn allowed the industrialization of Germany to take place on the basis of domestic food supplies. German farms could feed the massed populations of the new industrial towns with potatoes, as they could not have done with bread, simply because potatoes produced so many more calories per acre.

Before the 1880s, when railroads and steamships brought American grain to the European market in quantity, this was the only way the growing German population could have been fed. Hence it is no exaggeration to say that the swift rise of industrial Germany was the greatest political monument to the impact of American food crops on Europe—and on other continents as well, for World Wars I and II were among the consequences of that rise.

THE GREAT HUNGER: IRELAND 1845–1849

Cecil Woodham-Smith

The Great Hunger: Ireland 1845–1849 by Cecil Woodham-Smith is a history of the Irish potato famine. Her book draws heavily on primary sources as it explores the effects of this major economic and social tragedy. This reading is a letter by Nicholas Cummins, the magistrate of Cork, Ireland, sent to the Duke of Wellington in London. It describes Cummins's visit to Skibbereen on December 15, 1846. The letter was published in a London newspaper on December 24, 1846. As a result of the potato famine, hundreds of thousands of Irish emigrated, most of them to North America.

"My Lord Duke," wrote Mr. Cummins, "Without apology or preface, I presume so far to trespass on your Grace as to state to you, and by the use of your illustrious name, to present to the British public the following statement of what I have myself seen within the last three days. Having for many years been intimately connected with the western portion of the County of Cork, and possessing some small property there, I thought it right personally to investigate the truth of several lamentable accounts which had reached me, of the appalling state of misery to which that part of the country was reduced. I accordingly went on the 15th instant to Skibbereen, and to give the instance of one townland which I visited, as an example of the state of the entire coast district, I shall state simply what I there saw. . . . Being aware that I should have to witness scenes of frightful hunger, I provided myself with as much bread as five men could carry and on reaching the spot I was surprised to find the wretched hamlet apparently deserted. I entered some of the hovels to ascertain the cause, and the scenes which presented themselves were such as no tongue or pen can convey the

Searching for potatoes in a field.

slightest idea of. In the first, six famished and ghastly skeletons, to all appearances dead, were huddled in a corner on some filthy straw, their sole covering what seemed a ragged horse-cloth, their wretched legs hanging about, naked above the knees. I approached with horror, and found by a low moaning they were alive—they were in fever, four children, a woman and what had once been a man. It is impossible to go through the detail. Suffice it to say, that in a few minutes I was surrounded by at least 200 such phantoms, such frightful spectres as no words can describe, either from famine or from fever. Their demoniac yells are still ringing in my ears, and their horrible images are fixed upon my brain. My heart sickens at the recital, but I must go on.

"In another case, decency would forbid what follows, but it must be told. My clothes were nearly torn off in my endeavour to escape from the throng of pestilence around, when my neck-cloth was seized from behind by a grip which compelled me to turn, I found myself grasped by a woman with an infant just born in her arms and the remains of a filthy sack across her loins—the sole covering of herself and baby. The same morning the police opened a house on the adjoining lands, which was observed shut for many days, and two frozen corpses were found, lying upon the mud floor, half devoured by rats.

"A mother, herself in a fever, was seen the same day to drag out the corpse of her child, a girl about twelve, perfectly naked, and leave it half covered with stones. In another house, within 500 yards of the cavalry station at Skibbereen, the dispensary [a place where medical aid is given] doctor found seven wretches lying unable to move, under the same cloak. One had been dead many hours, but the others were unable to move either themselves or the corpse."

ONE HAPPY ENDING

Thomas Gallagher

Conditions were desperate for several years after the potato blight struck Ireland in 1845, forcing thousands to leave. Thomas Gallagher, author of Paddy's Lament, *tells one couple's story of leaving Ireland for America.*

For one eloping couple, a boy and girl running away to America, the pressure and suspense leading up to departure created a crisis that unalterably changed their lives. They had been driven to their embarkation point by a young man named Micky Quinn. The forty-mile trip had carried them through quiet farming country to this noisy, overcrowded seaport, where everything different and strange excited the young girl but confused and frightened the young man.

"Sure enough," he said, "the more I see of this, the less I want to see."

"It's not thinking of going back home you are, is it?" asked Dolores Kinsella, the girl eloping with him.

When the young man hesitated, Micky Quinn tried to urge him on with a bit of encouragement and hope. "God save you from temptation, Terry, and may you never button an empty pocket."

But with his imagination full of exaggerated visions of New York, Terry reneged and said he could not leave Ireland. Dolores and Micky looked at him, astonishment giving way to embarrassment and pain on both their faces. . . .

"By Him that made me, I'll go alone if I must," said Dolores, a black-haired teen-ager with Spanish in her blood and steel in her gray-green eyes.

Something like agony twisted and distorted the young man's face; he moved his arms and legs in odd, unnatural ways, while Dolores and Micky, friends since childhood, watched and waited. . . .

Several seconds passed, until Micky Quinn, whether to end the torture or take advantage of an unusual opportunity, found

As you read:
- **What kinds of events make people willing to leave their country?**
- **What fears do you think new immigrants have when they enter a new country?**

a solution. He suggested that he take the ticket and give the young man the horse and cart to return to the Glen, from which they had come.

Micky, an illiterate dressed only in a homespun jersey, knickers, and his dead father's old shoes, boarded the ship with Dolores. On arrival in New York, she would join her married sister in the city's infamous Five Points section around Mulberry Street on the Lower East Side, and he would gravitate to Greenpoint, Brooklyn, to land a job in a tavern and learn to read and write. But they would keep in touch with each other, off and on at first, then more often the more he learned to write. In two years they would be married. . . . Micky and Dolores would have six children, each one as real and delightful as their boarding the ship together had been unforeseen. Eventually, Micky would come to own the tavern and send home to Ireland for a footing of turf [earth]. When it arrived he would place it, by itself and without a word of explanation, in the middle of the tavern's window.

"No Irishman ever passed without going in," a friend would recall many years later. "The piece of the old sod did it. Sure, Micky had whips of money after being away twenty years. . . . a man who couldn't read or write when he left." There was a saying in those days, and it's as true today as it was then: "the only part of Ireland where a man can get ahead is in America."

Immigrants arriving in New York City.

SEEDS • OF • CHANGE

PRAISE THE POTATO!

Jack Denton Scott

As the potato spread throughout the world, it was not immediately accepted as a useful food. Today we know that the potato is one of the most nutritional food sources available to humans. It has become one of the world's most valuable foods. Jack Denton Scott presents a short history of the potato, discusses its nutritional value, and introduces the possibility that the potato could be used to wipe out world hunger.

The potato in America is served with more false beliefs than butter. Its true character is so clouded that we automatically place it in the same put-on-pounds category as chocolate cake and banana splits, convinced that it is long on starch, fat and carbohydrates, short on protein and vitamins.

But the truth is we would have to eat 11 pounds of potatoes to put on one pound of weight. Ounce for ounce, a boiled, medium-size potato, at only 76 calories, has no more calories than the keep-the-doctor-away apple, and fewer than cottage cheese, avocados, rice or bran flakes. What's more, though we spend only two percent of our food dollar on potatoes, we receive from that small amount our most economical, nutritionally balanced, staple food. The U.S. Department of Agriculture reports that if a person's entire diet consisted of potatoes, he would get all the riboflavin (B[2]), 1½ times the iron, three to four times the thiamin (B[1]) and niacin (B[3]) and more than ten times the amount of vitamin C that the body needs.

None of these facts were known to Peru's Inca Indians, who first cultivated the potato in about 200 B.C. Millions throughout the world are indebted to that culture—and to the looting Spanish conquistadors who in 1537 first found the potato in the Andean village of Sorocota.

Ranging in size from a nut to an apple, in color from gold and red to gray, blue and black, the strange vegetable of the Incas had many uses. Raw slices were placed on broken bones, rubbed on the head to cure aching, carried to prevent rheumatism, and eaten with other food to prevent indigestion. The Incas even knew how to preserve their staple food indefinitely. The potatoes were taken to 13,000 feet in the Andes, where they froze at night, then thawed in the sunlight. This process was repeated until the potatoes were without moisture, hard but very light—the world's first freeze-dried food.

The Incas' general name for this miracle plant of 52 varieties was *papa*, meaning tuber. The Spaniards preferred to call it *turma de tierra*, or truffle. They found it "floury, of good flavor, a dainty dish even for Spaniards."

But when they introduced the potato to Europe some 400 years ago, it immediately became the victim of myths and slander. Since it is not mentioned in the Bible, it was thought to be unfit for human use. And because it was not grown from seed, it was said to be evil, responsible for leprosy, syphilis and scrofula. French experts claimed it would destroy the soil in which it was planted, and physicians there said it was responsible for several serious illnesses and was a dangerous aphrodisiac.

It took at least two centuries after its export from South America for potatoes to be accepted and developed in Europe. England, for instance, did not produce them in any quantity until 1796 (though earlier, probably in 1663, that country did send some to Ireland where they were promptly planted and appreciated).

The United States got its first potatoes in 1719 when a colony of Irish settled at Londonderry, N.H. But even here potatoes were slow to win favor. As late as 1740, masters advised apprentices that they were not obliged to use potatoes, which were said to shorten men's lives. It was only after a few of the upper class pronounced them palatable that the new vegetable became popular.

It even took nutritionists a long time to rally around the potato. However, within the last few years they have been preaching that potatoes not only are a good source of essential amino acids, but are also high in potassium—a valuable aid in treating digestive disorders.

In addition, the potato gives excellent nutritional return for every gram of carbohydrate it contains. It is such a near-perfect food that the Agricultural Research of the U.S. Department of Agriculture has declared that "a diet of whole milk and potatoes would supply almost all of the food elements necessary for maintenance of the human body."

The tubers, or roots, are the only edible parts of a potato plant. One plant yields between three and twenty potatoes.

Noted nutritionist Jean Mayer says that people are obsessed with the idea that starchy foods are "horribly" fattening. Yet the fact is that the potato has fewer calories than believed and contains good-quality, easily digestible protein in ten percent of every 100 calories. Nutrition research studies indicate that

How to Buy, Store, and Cook Potatoes

Potatoes are classified by shape, skin color and use. The long brownish ones are good for a variety of uses, but best for baking. Round or long whites are preferred for boiling and baking, and the round reds are ideal for boiling. "New" potatoes, the small ones that are dug early before the skins have set, are best boiled or steamed. All potatoes can be used in any way you prefer, but the bakers usually are mealy and dry, the boilers moist and firm.

Select loose potatoes that are well formed, smooth, firm, with few eyes, no discoloration, cracks, bruises, or soft spots. Red potatoes and some whites are sometimes treated with colored or clear wax to make them appear fresher than they are. Avoid them. The FDA requires that those be plainly marked. Also, avoid "green" potatoes. They have been overexposed to light and have a bitter taste.

Do not wash potatoes before storing. Washing speeds decay. Potatoes can be safely stored in a dry, dark place for three months at 45 to 50 degrees Fahrenheit. Buy only a week's supply if you must store them at higher temperatures, which cause sprouting and shriveling.

Do not store potatoes in the refrigerator. Below 40 degrees, potato starch turns to sugar, making the potato too sweet. Too-cold storage also darkens the potatoes during cooking.

Bake, boil or steam them in their skins. Some nutrients close to the skin are lost when potatoes are peeled before cooking. If you must peel them, use a vegetable parer and peel as thinly as possible. Do not soak peeled potatoes in cold water to crisp them, since some nutrients will dissolve in the water.

How much nutrition in a potato?

Serving size: 1 medium potato (150 grams) about 1/3 pound

Calories	110
Protein	3 grams
Carbohydrate	23 grams
Fat	0 grams
Dietary Fiber	2710mg.
Sodium	10 mg.
Potassium	750 mg.

Percentage of U.S. Recommended Daily Allowances (U.S. RDA)

Protein	6
Vitamin C	50
Thiamin	8
Riboflavin	2
Niacin	10
Iron	8
Vitamin B	15
Folacin (folic acid)	8
Phosphorus	8
Magnesium	8
Zinc	2
Copper	8
Pantothenic acid	4
Iodine	15

Source: *The Potato Board*

when starch, as in potatoes, is substituted for sugar in the diet, appetite is lessened. Bulky, packed with vitamins and minerals, potatoes are valuable in a balanced reducing diet.

Even of fried potatoes ten ½ x ½ x 2-inch slices amount to just 137 calories. Compare that with the 300 calories for a hamburger or two hot-dogs, 420 for a piece of chocolate cake, 200 for a doughnut, or even the 225 calories for a cup of cooked rice, and compute the relative food values. The potato comes out far ahead in its balance of nutrients.

Although it is hard to beat that easy standby, the baked potato drenched in butter, Americans keep trying. We blend the mealy baking potatoes with everything from cottage cheese to caviar and salmon. We also hash, mash, mince, cream, fry, steam, boil and roast potatoes; add them to soups and chowders; team them with tuna; couple them with chicken; even make delicious doughnuts and chocolate cake with them. We also invented potato chips, and produce four billion pounds just to satisfy the average American's appetite for 4½ pounds per annum.

Still, our most popular potato dish was invented by the French. But the French, who fondly call the potato *pomme de terre,* "apple of the earth," do much more than "French fry" them. They have over 100 classic recipes, from the dramatic *pommes de terre soufflées* which puff into hollow golden balls, to the impressive *pommes Anna,* sliced very thin, baked in sweet butter and turned out like a cake.

The Germans have two names for the potato: *kartoffel,* or truffle, and *erdapfel,* earth apple. They use it for noodles, dumplings, pancakes and bread; imaginatively mix mashed potatoes with applesauce, sugar and vinegar; use potatoes to stuff geese; and make a renowned hot potato salad. The Italians turn the *patate* into their famous *gnocchi* [dumplings]. The Spanish fill a spectacular omelette with *papas,* the Greeks make a superb sauce, *skordalia,* with potato, olive oil, garlic and lemon.

The world's ways with the potato are endless, but its first producers, the Peruvians, may have the most imaginative touch. They have created the lusty, justly famous *causa a la limena*—mashed potatoes mixed with lemon juice, olive oil, chopped onions, salt, pepper and spine-stiffening hot chili peppers.

The poor man's food and the gourmet's delight also has, historically, come full circle in the country of its origin. In La

Modern-day potato products.

Molina, Peru, at the International Potato Center, 86 scientists from 23 countries are creating "Super Spud." Their objective: to perfect a potato that will grow fast in the humid tropics where millions of the hungriest poor live. The plan is for Super Spud not only to become an important food source in those areas where it is presently unknown, but to have its rapid growth prevent storage problems.

The Center's scientists have advanced to the point of developing Super Spud into edible tubers in 31 days, maturity in 60 days (an Idaho or Maine potato takes 120 days). Right now they are working on the last obstacle: a completely disease-resistant potato for the poor farmers in the tropics who have no pesticides available, and couldn't afford them if they did.

Thus, the humble vegetable from Peru may soon leave its homeland on its second and most important journey—to wipe out world hunger.

THE HORSE
RETURN OF A NATIVE

In 1493, when Columbus sailed to the Americas for the second time, he brought horses with him. The horse, a native of the Americas, was returning home after an absence of 10,000 years. For millions of years, ancestors of the horse had roamed North and South America. During the Ice Age, many horses had migrated to Asia across the Bering land bridge. The remaining horses had gradually disappeared from the American continents.

In the several hundred years following its return, the horse would radically change the lives of American Indians—first by helping the Spanish conquistadors conquer and control the Indians and later by becoming an important part of Indian life.

SEEDS • OF • CHANGE

Taming the Horse

Horses that had crossed the Bering land bridge from the Americas roamed the grasslands of Asia and Europe. Scientists think that people living near the Volga River in Eastern Europe first domesticated horses about 6,000 years ago. The horse provided humans with speed and power in transportation. It helped carry loads, plow fields, hunt game, and fight enemies. In time, migrants from Eastern Europe shared their four-legged treasures with people in China and Mongolia in Asia. From there, the horse traveled with its human companions to areas around the Mediterranean Sea.

Along the Mediterranean coast in northern Africa, the Moslem people, called Moors, became especially good horse

Spanish horses being unloaded from a ship in the Americas.

breeders and riders. When they crossed the Mediterranean to invade Spain in the early 700s A.D., they took their horses with them. Horses gave them the advantage they needed to defeat the Spanish.

The Moors' victory convinced the Spanish of the horse's value. Over the next several hundred years, the Spanish became the most skilled horse breeders and riders of Europe. Spanish horses became the finest of their kind. Crossbreeding the strong, fast horse of Spain and the fine Arabian horses introduced by the Moors produced large, nicely formed horses that performed well in war, mounted games, and racing.

Horses became plentiful and inexpensive in Spain. As a result, members of all classes could view the world from horseback. By 1492, when they finally drove out the Moors, the Spanish were Europe's finest horsemen. Having fought and won wars with their cavalry, or mounted soldiers, the Spanish were well aware of the value of horses in military conflict. As instruments of war, horses were enormously successful in the early years of the Spanish conquest.

Horses in the Americas

The horses hoisted off the ships at Hispaniola in 1493 were far different from the ancestors that had trotted to Asia and Europe 10,000 years before. *Eohippus*, the oldest known horse, was no larger than a fox terrier, with a humped spine, short legs, and toes—four on the front feet, three on the back. Thousands of years of evolution and hundreds of years of breeding had transformed the tiny creature. The horse coming home to the Americas was an impressive, handsome animal with a solid body and a high arched neck. Its spine and legs were long and straight, and it was an efficient runner.

American Indians had never seen horses. They were awed by the animal's size, strength, speed, and obedience to humans. The presence of just a few horses on Hispaniola so frightened the Arawak Indians that Columbus had little trouble subduing them. After this first military success, Columbus demanded that horses be included on every ship leaving for the Americas. One conquistador said, "Horses are the most necessary thing for the new country because they frighten the enemy most, and, after God, to them belongs the victory."

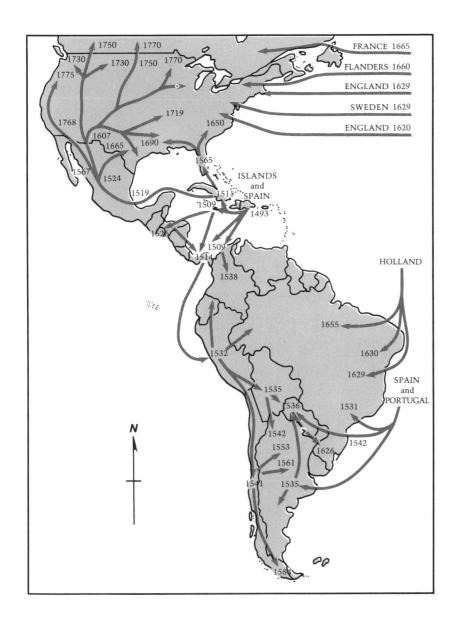

The following labels appear on the map:

1750 1770
1730 1730 1750 1770
1775
1768 1719
1607 1650
1665 1690
1567 1565
1524
1519 1511
1509
1493
1626
1509
1514
1538

FRANCE 1665
FLANDERS 1660
ENGLAND 1629
SWEDEN 1629
ENGLAND 1620

ISLANDS
and
SPAIN

HOLLAND

1655
1630
1629

SPAIN
and
PORTUGAL

1532
1535
1536 1531
1542 1542
1553 1626
1561
1541 1535
1589

N

The Spread of the Horse in North and South America

As the Caribbean islands became the launching bases for explorations onto the South and North American continents, European settlers in the islands began raising horses for the explorers to take with them. Explorers no longer had to bring horses from Europe. They were assured of good, healthy horses to take with them to the American mainlands. When Hernán Cortés began his assault on Mexico in 1519, he and his men rode horses bred in Cuba. The Aztecs in Mexico were as unfamiliar with the horse as the Arawaks had been.

Spanish conquistador and historian Bernal Díaz reported that when some Aztecs first saw a mounted conquistador, they thought the rider and horse were one beast. The Aztecs quickly learned that rider and horse were separate. The Aztecs also realized the great advantage horses gave the Spanish soldiers. Along with smallpox, horses became an enemy of the Aztecs as they attempted to save their empire from the Spanish conquerors.

Horses brought to the mainland multiplied as rapidly as they did on the Caribbean islands. By 1550, horses were so plentiful in the region around Mexico City that, to obtain a mount, all a Spaniard had to do was rope one. As the Spanish frontier moved into northern Mexico and south to Central America, the number of horses increased. By the early 1600s, according to reports, wild horses too numerous to count ran the length of Mexican lands.

Horses in South America

Francisco Pizarro brought horses to aid him in conquering Peru in the 1530s. Herds spread from there south into Chile and then onto the vast *pampas* of Argentina and Uruguay. On these endless grasslands, the horse population seemed to explode, and, soon, many South American nomadic Indian tribes adopted the horse.

Before the arrival of the horse, these Indians had chased camel-like guanacos and other wild game on foot and captured them with *bolas,* long ropes with heavy rocks tied to each end. A hunter swung a bola over his head until it was spinning, then released it in full swing. Striking the animal, the bola wrapped around its legs and prevented it from running away.

After the Spanish arrived in South America, the pampas hunters began to use both horses and the Spanish *lazo,* or lasso, along with bolas in their hunting. These roaming cowboys, often of mixed Spanish and Indian ancestry, became known as *gauchos.*

Great changes occurred in the life-styles of Indians who took to horseback. They expanded their hunting and gathering territories, and their increased food supply fueled population growth. Expansion brought Indians into frequent collisions over territory. New leaders emerged. Leadership no longer came from tribal elders but passed instead to mounted warriors who distinguished themselves in battle.

SEEDS • OF • CHANGE

South American gauchos hunt guanacos with bolas.

Raids against the Spaniards or other Indian tribes became common events.

The Horse and the North American Indians

Within a few years of Cortés's victory, Spanish explorers were traveling north by horseback into the deserts and plains of North America. They often looted and killed Indians along the way. Because they were often easily defeated in battle by mounted Spaniards, Indians quickly realized the value of owning horses.

Knowing that the horse was one of their most powerful weapons, the Spanish tried to keep Indians from owning horses. Some Indians, however, captured runaway horses and stole others. Other Indians traded with *commancheros*, people of half-Spanish and half-Indian descent, exchanging Indian goods in return for horses.

Over time, Indians learned to breed horses. Some became cowboys, or *vaqueros*. These were Indians who lived in California or Mexico missions, set up to Christianize native people. Many were part of the Spanish *encomienda* system, which began in the early 1500s. Under the *encomienda* system, a group of Indians was assigned to a conquistador or other privileged colonist. The colonist was allowed to use the Indians as laborers but was expected to care for them and teach them Christian ways. In practice, the Indians were often treated as slaves.

In 1680, pueblo Indians living near Santa Fe, New Mexico, rose up against the Spanish foreigners who had treated them badly. During this uprising, known as the Pueblo Revolt, Indians massacred Spanish settlers and captured or freed thousands of horses. The freed horses probably began the first herds of mustangs and other wild horses in the West.

The Pueblo Revolt eventually changed the lives of most Indian tribes throughout the North American West and Great Plains. As South American Indians had discovered in the pampas, North American Plains Indians found that with horses they could expand their hunting grounds. They could more easily move their people and belongings from camp to camp is search of better food supplies. They could hunt buffalo more efficiently on horseback than on foot, and they could better fight their enemies—both other Indians and the encroaching Europeans. For tribes that acquired guns from Europeans at about the same time they got horses, warfare became more frequent and more violent.

Less than 100 years after the Pueblo Revolt, the Great Plains were filled with hard-riding warriors on horseback from such legendary buffalo-hunting tribes as the Blackfoot, Arapaho, Cheyenne, Crow, Sioux, and Comanche. Horses became prized possessions, and as such were the subject of Indian art and legend. Indians wove horse images into blankets and baskets and painted them on hides and rock walls. The horse also appeared often in their myths and legends.

Cattle, Cowboys, and the Horse
Along with horses from their homeland, the Spanish brought to the Americas longhorned cattle and a knowledge of cattle ranching. The Spanish established their first cattle ranches in Mexico on Aztec lands during the 1500s. Other Spanish settlers began ranches in present-day California, Arizona, New Mexico, Texas, and Florida in the 1600s. They turned both cattle and horses loose on the grasslands of North America. The herds multiplied, taking over more and more Indian homelands. The Spanish, in effect, were responsible for starting the "cowboy era."

Pioneers moving into the Texas territory in the 1800s often became cattle ranchers. They adopted both the tough Spanish longhorn cattle and the Spanish ranching system. The cattle ranchers adopted Spanish ranching equipment and dress. Spanish *chaparejos* became the American "chaps," or leather trousers. The Spanish *la reata* became the American "lariat," or cowboy's rope. The Spanish *vaquero* became the American "buckaroo," or cowboy.

After the American Civil War ended in 1865, cattle ranching spread across the Great Plains into Oklahoma, Kansas, Nebraska, and Missouri. Longhorns roamed unfenced lands until butchering time. Railroads were built to transport cattle from cattle towns like Dodge City and Kansas City to cities in the East.

The horse became as much a symbol of the cowboy as it did of the Indian. For about 25 years, cowboys on horseback rounded up and herded thousands of cattle across hundreds of miles from Texas and New Mexico to the cattle towns. This period became known as the golden age of cowboys, who later became the heroes of American western movies.

The golden age ended in the late 1800s. Inventions such as the steel plow and the windmill allowed ranchers to plant, irrigate, and harvest corn for cattle feed. Barbwire fences kept cattle in smaller areas, eliminating the need for big roundups. Railroads were extended farther and farther into cattle country, making annual roundups and cattle

This Indian rock painting in Canyon de Chelly National Monument shows the coming of the Europeans on horseback.

drives unnecessary. In the heartland of North America, European cattle and Central American corn came together to create the world's largest livestock industry, and most cowboys found themselves out of work.

The Horse Today

For nearly 6,000 years after its domestication, the horse played a critical role in human life. Horses were bred, roped, harnessed, ridden, spurred, and raced. Horses carried heavy loads, plowed fields, and accompanied their masters into battle.

With the coming of the train and, later, the automobile, the horse's role in the Americas changed. Engines replaced horse power with machine power. Most of the horse's ranch and farming jobs were gradually taken over by machines.

Today, people use horses mostly for recreation. Horses and their riders compete in races, shows, and rodeos. Many families enjoy horses as pets. Whatever its role in the future, the horse's role in the past has left an unforgettable mark on the history of the American continents.

Bill Pickett

Bill Pickett: Famous Steer Wrestler

Modern-day rodeo grew out of the skills cowboys and cowgirls used during the 1800s. In a rodeo, contestants match their skills in bronco riding, bull riding, roping, and steer wrestling, also called bulldogging. In this event, a cowboy, riding full speed next to a steer, jumps from the horse to the steer's back. The cowboy grabs the steer by the head and horns, plants his feet on the ground to stop, and throws the steer to the ground. A winner in this event takes the least amount of time to accomplish this feat. A famous bulldogger in the late 1890s was Bill Pickett, one of the many African American cowboys of the period. Pickett is sometimes credited with inventing bulldogging.

VICTORY AT CINTLA

Bernal Díaz

Bernal Díaz del Castillo (c.1492–c.1581) was the last survivor of the conquerors of Mexico. He served as a soldier during Cortés's conquest of the Aztec capital, Tenochtitlán. Díaz writes with first-hand knowledge of military actions. Although he did not write The Conquest of New Spain *until his old age, his memory of the events was vivid. In the following selection, Díaz reports on the first battle Cortés fought in Mexico. He describes the brutality of war and the importance of the horse in Spanish conquest.*

As soon as Cortés knew that the Indians intended to attack, he ordered all the horses to be quickly landed, and the crossbowmen, musketeers, and the rest of us soldiers, including even the wounded, to have our arms ready for use.

When the horses came ashore they were very stiff and afraid to move, for they had been on board for some time. Next day, however, they moved quite freely. . . .

The best horses and riders were chosen to form the cavalry, and little bells were attached to the horses' breastplates. The horsemen were ordered not to stop and spear those who were down, but to aim their lances at the faces of the enemy.

Thirteen gentlemen were chosen to go on horseback, with Cortés as their commander. Mesa the artilleryman was ordered to have his guns ready, and Diego de Ordaz was given the command of all us footsoldiers, musketeers, and crossbowmen, for he was no horseman.

Very early next morning, which was Lady Day [a feast day that honors the mother of Jesus Christ], after hearing Fray Bartolome de Olmedo say mass, we all formed up behind our standard-bearer, who was at the time Antonio de Villaroel, and marched to the same wide savannah [treeless plain], about three miles from the camp, where Francisco de Lugo and Pedro de Alvarado had been attacked. This place was called Cintla, as was the near-by town, which was subject to Tabasco.

Aztec drawing showing a battle between Aztecs and horse-mounted Spanish conquistadors.

As we marched along, separated by some distance from Cortés and his horsemen, on account of swamps which the horses could not cross, we fell in with a whole force of Indian warriors on their way to attack us in our camp. It was near this same town of Cintla that we met them on the open plain, and if these warriors were seeking us with battle in their minds, we had the same thoughts in seeking them.

When we met the enemy bands and companies which we had marched out to find, they were, as I have said, coming in search of us. All the men wore great feather crests, they carried drums and trumpets, their faces were painted black and white, they were armed with large bows and arrows, spears and shields, swords like our two-handed swords, and slings and stones and fire-toughened darts, and all wore quilted cotton armor. Their squadrons, as they approached us, were so numerous that they covered the whole savannah. They rushed on us like mad dogs and completely surrounded us, discharging such a rain of arrows, darts, and stones upon us that more than

SEEDS • OF • CHANGE

seventy of our men were wounded at the first attack. Then, in the hand-to-hand fighting, they did us great damage with their spears. One soldier was killed outright by an arrow-wound in the ear, and they kept on shooting and wounding us. With our muskets and crossbows and good sword-play we put up a stout fight, and once they came to feel the edge of our swords they gradually fell back, but only to shoot at us from greater safety. Our artilleryman Mesa killed many of them with his cannon. For since they came in great bands and did not open out, he could fire at them as he pleased. But with all the hurts and wounds we dealt them, we could not drive them off. . . .

I remember that whenever we fired our guns, the Indians gave great shouts and whistles, and threw up straw and earth so that we could not see what harm we had done them. They sounded their trumpets and drums, and shouted and whistled, and cried, *Alala! Alala!*

Just at this moment we caught sight of our horsemen. But the great host of Indians was so crazed by their attack that they did not at once see them approaching behind their backs. As the plain was bare and the horsemen were good riders, and some of the horses were very swift and nimble, they came quickly upon them and speared them as they chose. As soon as we saw the horsemen we fell on the enemy so vigorously that, caught between the horsemen and ourselves, they soon turned tail. The Indians thought at that time that the horse and rider were one creature, for they had never seen a horse before. . . .

After the horsemen had dismounted beneath some trees beside which some houses stood, we returned thanks to God for granting us so complete a victory. Then, as it was Lady Day, we named the town which was afterwards founded here Santa Maria de la Victoria, on account of the fact that this great victory was won on her day. This was the first battle that we fought under Cortés in New Spain.

MARES AND HORSES

Garcilaso de la Vega

Garcilaso de la Vega (1539–1616) was born in Cuzco, the ancient capital of the Incas in Peru. He was the son of a Spanish conquistador and an Incan princess. In this excerpt from his Royal Commentaries of the Incas (1609), *de la Vega tells how horses were tamed and used by conquistadors in the conquest of the Americas.*

In the first place, the Spaniards brought mares [female horses] and horses with them, and with their aid they completed the conquest of the New World; for the Indians, being born and bred in the country, are more agile than the Spaniards in flight and pursuit and in climbing up and down and running among the rough and craggy places of Peru. The race of horses found throughout all the Indian kingdoms and provinces that have been discovered and conquered by the Spaniards since the year 1492 is the Spanish breed, and more particularly, that of Andalusia. The first were taken to the islands of Cuba and Santo Domingo, and then to the other Windward Islands as these were discovered and conquered. Here they bred in great abundance, and were taken thence for the conquest of Mexico and Peru, etc. In the beginning, partly because of the neglect of their owners, and partly because of the almost incredible difficulty of the mountains there, some of the mares strayed into the wilderness and were lost. A great many of them were gradually lost in this way; and their owners, seeing that they bred freely in the mountains and came to no harm from wild beasts, even released tame animals to go with them. In this way the islands came to possess a race of wild horses that fled like deer from human beings, yet multiplied rapidly on account of the fertility of the country, which is hot and damp and never lacking in green grass.

When the Spaniards living in these islands saw that they needed horses for the conquests they thereafter undertook, and that this breed was a very good one, they began to raise them

This drawing from the 1600s shows a fully equipped Spanish cavalry soldier.

on their estates and were very well paid for them. There were men who had thirty, forty, or fifty horses in their stables. . . . In order to catch the colts they build wooden enclosures in the hills, along the paths by which the horses come and go to graze on the clearings. . . . The animals come out of the woods to pasture at certain hours, and watchers who are sitting up in the trees make a signal, whereupon fifteen or twenty men appear on horseback and drive the wild horses into the enclosures. Mares and colts are penned up indiscriminately. Then the three-year-old colts are lassoed and fastened to trees, and the mares let loose. The colts stay tied up for three or four days, and kick and leap until they are so tired and hungry that they cannot stand and some of them swoon. When their mettle [vigor] has been broken, they are saddled and reined, and mounted by youths, while others lead them by the halter. They are treated in this way night and morning for fifteen or twenty days until they are broken in. The colts, like animals bred for the express purpose of serving man, respond nobly and loyally to whatever he demands of them. . . . They turn out excellent mounts. More recently, as the number of new conquests has dropped off, the old style of horse breeding has disappeared, and farmers have taken to breeding cattle for their hides. . . .

THE HORSE CULTURE

Herman J. Viola

Herman J. Viola is director of Quincentenary Programs at the National Museum of Natural History, Smithsonian Institution. Dr. Viola is an expert on the American Indian and author of numerous books on the subject. In this selection from After Columbus: The Smithsonian Chronicle of North American Indians, *Viola provides great insight into the impact of the horse on the Indian way of life.*

As you read:
- **Why do you think the Spanish wanted to keep Indians from getting horses?**
- **How did horses and firearms change Indian cultures?**

The horse originated in what are now the Americas more than 40 million years ago. It became extinct in its homeland, but, unlike most species, it was able to make a comeback: dispersing from the New World to the Old via the then exposed land bridge to Siberia, it eventually reached Europe and, at the end of this roundabout route, the Spanish reintroduced the horse to America. In 1493, on his second voyage, Columbus brought horses back to the Western Hemisphere after an absence of 10,000 years.

Spain's *conquistadores* rode horses and used them effectively against the Indians they encountered, who were frightened of the "sky dogs," believing they were monsters or messengers of the gods. When the Hopis saw their first horses they paved their way with ceremonial blankets.

The Native Americans' awe of horses quickly gave way to a powerful urge to obtain these wonderful creatures, but the Spanish were equally desirous to keep them out of Indian hands. Nonetheless, by the late 1700s virtually every tribe in the Far West was mounted or at least had access to horses (some of the mountain tribes ate rather than rode theirs). Recent scholarship has revealed the probable routes and methods by which Indians of the Plains and the American Southwest obtained their mounts. This remarkable story highlights the trading acumen [cleverness] and adaptability of the American tribes. . . .

Historians once attributed the actual re-introduction of the horse to the Great Plains to 16th-century explorers Francisco

SEEDS • OF • CHANGE

Coronado and Hernando de Soto. It was thought that runaway mounts stocked the Plains with the great wild herds so familiar in the lore of the West. Subsequent research, however, has discredited this theory. Although both expeditions were well mounted—Coronado's, for instance, had 558 horses—these animals simply could not have been producing offspring, for Spanish law required soldiers to ride stallions. Only two of Coronado's horses were mares, and both returned to New Spain with him. It is now generally accepted that the Indians acquired their horses a century later from Spanish herds in New Mexico. Some they stole, but most they obtained as a result of the Pueblo Indian uprising of 1680. From New Mexico, horses moved rapidly north and east along established trading networks, although some were captured during intertribal raiding. However obtained, mounts represented wealth, status, power, and the ability to move people and goods with efficiency and speed.

The Lakota are typical of the tribes whose cultures were transformed by the horse. In the 1760s some Lakota were canoeing people of what is today Minnesota; within 30 years the western Lakota had become part of the greatest light cavalry

Before North American Indians began using horse-drawn travoises to carry supplies, they used dogs to pull smaller travoises.

history has ever known. The horse drew them toward the prairie, the gun drove them from canoe country.

The spread of horses from the West was nearly simultaneous with the introduction of firearms from the East, the latter allowing easterly tribes to push westerly people out onto the Plains. The guns arrived despite initial trade embargoes. As early as 1622, within two years of the arrival of the *Mayflower*, the Puritans petitioned the British Crown to pass the first law against supplying weapons to Indians, "upon Paine of our high Indignation," but such regulations proved almost impossible to enforce. By 1628, according to Plymouth Colony Governor William Bradford's reckoning, the Indians of New England owned more than 60 guns, with the number increasing every year. . . .

As the wars of empire intensified, suppliers profited mightily from the gun traffic. Colonies vied in this commerce, relaxing their laws so as not to be undercut in trade. Later, certain tribes located along strategic waterways, such as the Arikara, Hidatsa, and Mandan Indians, who lived in villages along the Missouri River, for a time enjoyed a thriving business as the middlemen of the complex trade network that moved horses east and guns west. The Crow Indians of the Yellowstone country were another such intermediary. They obtained horses and mules from their Flathead, Shoshone, and Nez Percé suppliers, and then exchanged the animals at the Hidatsa and Mandan villages for muskets, gunpowder, and lead.

So impersonal an economic force as trade can prove dramatic as its impact becomes evident at the human level. Imagine, for example, an Indian's shock at first confronting an enemy on a horse, or first fighting a warrior armed with a gun. Similarly, the confluence [junction] on the northern Plains of the two opposing streams of trade—where eastern and western routes met—provided a crucial impetus to American Indian history.

One witness to this fateful encounter was a Cree Indian named Saukamaupee, who during the winter of 1787–88 related his account to Hudson's Bay fur trader David Thompson. As a young man, Saukamaupee had lived with the Piegan Indians, who are Canadian relatives of the Blackfeet. The Piegans were continually at war with their Shoshone neighbors, and Saukamaupee participated in several conflicts. In a battle that took place about 1730, several Shoshones rode horses, which he

The Buffalo Hunt *by John Inness captures the excitement of this vital activity. The horse gave Indian hunters speed and mobility, two advantages they had lacked on foot.*

and his Piegan friends had never seen before. Swinging their stone war clubs, the mounted Shoshones charged and quickly routed the Piegans. To help fight their new overpowering enemy, the frightened Piegans sought assistance from their Assiniboine and Cree neighbors to the east, who did not have horses but who had obtained a revolutionary new weapon of their own, the "fire stick." The next time the two foes met, ten Cree and Assiniboine musketeers assisted the Piegans, and it was the surprised and terrified Shoshones who fled.

The Piegans soon got their first close look at a Shoshone horse, which had died from an arrow wound in its belly. "Numbers of us went to see him," Saukamaupee recalled, "and we all admired him; he put us in mind of a stag that had lost his horns, and we did not know what name to give him. But as he was a slave to Man, like the dog, which carried our things, he was named the Big Dog." Later, because horses were the size of elk, the Piegans began calling them *ponokomita,* or "elk dog," which remains their word for horse.

Such encounters were experienced over and over again, in tribe after tribe. . . . The new, highly effective combination of mobility and firepower fueled a startling social and technological revolution among Indian peoples, one that predestined the violent encounter that would erupt between whites and Indians as American settlers began to stream west to claim Indian lands.

THE WAR GOD'S HORSE SONG

The horse changed almost every dimension of Indian culture. Its influence was reflected in ritual and poetry. "The War God's Horse Song" is an example of Navajo oral tradition—the passing on of stories or poetry by talking or singing.

I am the Turquoise Woman's son.
On top of Belted Mountain
Beautiful horses—slim like a weasell
My horse has a hoof like striped agate;
His fetlock is like a fine eagle plume;
His legs are like quick lightning.
My horse's body is like an eagle-plumed arrow;
My horse has a tail like a trailing black cloud.
I put flexible goods on my horse's back;
The Little Holy Wind blows through his hair.

His mane is made of short rainbows.
My horse's ears are made of round corn.
My horse's eyes are made of big stars.
My horse's head is made of mixed waters
(From the holy waters—he never knows thirst).
My horse's teeth are made of white shell.
The long rainbow is in his mouth for a bridle,
    And with it I guide him.
When my horse neighs, different-colored horses follow.
When my horse neighs, different-colored sheep follow.
    I am wealthy, because of him.
    Before me peaceful,
    Behind me peaceful,
    Under me peaceful,
    Over me peaceful,
    All around me peaceful—
    Peaceful voice when he neighs.

A FRONTIERSWOMAN ON A MONTANA RANCH

Nannie T. Alderson

Nannie T. Alderson was born in 1860 into the southern aris-
tocracy on a slave-holding plantation in Virginia. In 1882, she
and her husband, Walt, moved to southeastern Montana to
establish their first ranch. Her memoirs, A Bride Goes West
(1942), were transcribed and co-authored by Helena
Huntington Smith when Nannie Alderson was 82 years old. It
remains one of the finest records of a woman's life on the
Montana frontier. In this selection, Alderson describes the role
of the horse in ranch life.

Raising cattle never was like working on a farm. It was always
uncertain and exciting—you had plenty of money or you were
broke—and then, too, work on horseback, while dangerous and
often very hard, wasn't drudgery. There was more freedom to it.
Even we women felt that, though the freedom wasn't ours.

  To me at first ranch life had endless novelty and fascination.
There were horses to be broken and cattle to be branded, because new ones that we bought had to have our mark of ownership put on them before they were turned out on the range.
Something was always going on in the corral, and I would leave
the dishes standing in the kitchen and run down and watch,
sometimes for hours. This having a Wild West show in one's
own back yard was absorbing but it was terrifying; I never
could get used to the sight, but would marvel how anyone
could stay on such a wild, twisting, plunging mass of horse-
flesh. The boys took it all quite calmly, and would call to the
rider to "Stay with him!" as though it were just a show. My
husband always rode the ones that bucked the hardest. It was
awful to see his head snap as if his neck would break, yet I
never could stay away. . . .

As you read:
• How would you
  describe the role of
  women on a Montana
  frontier ranch? How
  do you think the lives
  of ranch women are
  different today?

*A broncobuster tames a
wild horse in 1904.*

Sometimes the boys would run races on their favorite horses, and I would hold the stakes. I often went riding when I ought to have been at work. I had a dark blue broadcloth riding habit, with a trailing skirt, and a tightly fitted coat made á la militaire, with three rows of brass buttons down the front. The buttons were a gift from a cousin who went to Annapolis, but was expelled along with two or three other Southern boys for hazing [harassing] a negro midshipman [naval academy student]. My riding habit was even more inappropriate to the surroundings than the rest of my clothes. But the men liked it, and there were no women around to criticize.

My mounts were a chapter in themselves. Gentle horses, as the term is understood in more civilized parts, were almost as rare in Montana as kangaroos. Therefore it was a routine operation, when I was going riding, for one of the boys to get on the horse first with my side saddle and skirt and "take the buck out of him," after which I would get on and ride off, trusting to Providence that he was through for the day. All cowboys, wherever they worked, had each his "string" of eight or ten horses, which actually belonged to the company but which were regarded as the sacred private property of the man who rode them. What was referred to as my "string" consisted of one elderly bay cow pony known as Old Pete. Old Pete was neither good-looking nor a lady's saddle horse, but he was considered gentle because he didn't buck except on starting out, and he would tolerate a side saddle. One day, however, Brown [a ranch hand] remarked with a thoughtful expression: "I'm afraid Old Pete's going to blow up with you some day when you're riding him. He did it with me."

If he did "blow up" I knew what would happen, but at the time it was Old Pete or nothing. When the roundup came, however, I acquired a new and safer mount.

Many young people have told me how they envied the freedom of the unfenced range as we knew it. But I fear that to the girls of today we should have seemed very quaint. Being married, I felt like a mother to the bachelors, even when they were older than I was, and none of them ever called me by my first name. As for Mr. Alderson, I never could bring myself to call him "Walt," the way the boys did. We didn't do that, in the South. Back home you would hear women say: "Why, I couldn't call my husband George"—or William or Henry. "You'd call a servant by his first name!" Of course I couldn't

SEEDS • OF • CHANGE

address my husband as I would a servant—not even in Montana where there were no servants! I believe we stuck all the more firmly to our principles of etiquette, because we were so far from civilization. We could still stand on ceremony, even though our floors were dirt. . . .

The boys were always scrupulous [careful] about swearing where I could hear them. But when they were working in the corral, they would forget that the wind could carry the sound up to the house. I caught nearly all of them that way at one time or another. Once I even caught Mr. Alderson. It was one day in the summer while they were finishing the new house. I had taken my darning and gone over there to sit, as I often did—because it was cooler there, and one of our new chairs, still done up in burlap, made a comfortable seat. A half-finished partition hid me from Mr. Alderson and Hal, who were working on the tongued-and-grooved ceiling. This was a difficult piece of work, and when Hal, in his irresponsible way, dropped his end of a board and tore out the whole groove, Mr. Alderson swore at him just terribly. I hated so to hear him, I dropped my work and ran to the shack—greatly to the delight of that scamp Hal.

A Montana pioneer, 1909. Many women ran or helped run ranches and had to be skilled at handling horses.

SUGAR
A SWEET TOOTH LEADS TO SLAVERY

Contained in the cargo that Columbus and his crew unloaded at Hispaniola in 1493 were cuttings of sugarcane plants. Sugarcane would grow well in the Caribbean islands, but it would also prove to be the cause of one of the cruelest chapters in the world's history.

The Demand for Sugar

Sugar may be the most popular food ever discovered. No one who has known sweet foods has ever completely rejected them. Some experts believe that sweetness may have been an indication to earliest humans that a food was safe to eat. Whatever the reason, humans seem to have a built-in liking for sweet tastes.

Plantation slaves cutting cane.

Sugar is not a necessary requirement for the human diet. In fact, eating too much sugar can be harmful. It may be a factor in weight gain, tooth decay, and some health problems. Some experts contend that sugar, after illegal drugs, tobacco, and alcohol, is the most damaging substance craved by humans.

Table sugar, as well as the sugar added to many foods, is called *sucrose.* Sucrose comes from the juice in sugarcane and sugar beets. Through a complex manufacturing process, the juice is refined into the familiar small, white grains. The production of cane sugar has been around for about 10,000 years. However, it only has been widely consumed for about 400 years.

Sugar Demand in Europe

Until about 1,000 years ago, few northern Europeans knew about sugar. At that time, travelers returning from northern Africa and crusaders returning from the Middle East began to spread news about sugar throughout Europe. The Moors had brought sugarcane with them to Spain about A.D. 900. For several centuries, the sweetener continued to be a rare and expensive substance. Sugar became a status symbol, used by royalty and the very rich as medicine or a costly novelty food.

About A.D. 1600, use of sugar began to spread from Europe's upper classes to the common people. It became a special favorite in England, where it was used to sweeten coffee and cocoa, popular new drinks from the Americas, and tea imported from China. In the early 1800s, the British instituted an afternoon social event around these drinks that eventually included rich cakes, buns, and breads, all of which included sugar. Sugar became a common cooking ingredient in England and later throughout Europe. By the end of the 1600s, the European demand for sugar had become so great that a nation could become wealthy by simply producing and selling sugar to other countries.

Growing Sugarcane

Sugarcane is a grass whose mature stalks measure about twelve to fifteen feet high and two inches thick. Hundreds of years ago, hand cutting cane was a difficult, exhausting process. Once cut, the stalks had to be hurried to the sugar factory to be ground into juice as soon as possible. The process of grinding the stalks and heating the juice to a very high temperature created a liquid that was then refined into sugar. In the boiling houses where the juice was processed, the temperatures often rose above 120 degrees Fahrenheit. The planting, harvesting, and processing of sugar was backbreaking, dangerous work that required many laborers.

Sugar in the Americas

In 1516, the first Caribbean sugar shipment reached Europe from the island of Santa Domingo. The European demand for sugar grew year by year. To meet that demand, Europeans claimed huge areas of land in the Caribbean islands. They established sugar *plantations,* very large farms that needed hundreds of workers to plant crops and harvest them. By 1530, a dozen or more sugar plantations dotted the Caribbean.

The first European plantation owners had planned to enslave the American Indians to grow and process the sugarcane. However, many Indians died from contagious European diseases or from the foreigners' brutal treatment. Some, refusing to be enslaved, escaped or killed themselves. The plantation owners then turned to a workforce already employed by the Spanish and Portuguese on their Atlantic island plantations—enslaved West Africans.

Slavery, the ownership of humans by other humans, was considered essential to the plantation system's success. It provided a seemingly inexhaustible, free supply of labor. Slave traders, called *slavers*, turned their attention to the demand for slaves in the Caribbean.

In less than 100 years after Columbus's second voyage, the Caribbean and northern South America had become the prime sugar-producing region in the world. Europeans came from England, France, Portugal, and the Netherlands to build sugar plantations. By 1700, 80 percent of Europe's sugar came from the Caribbean islands. Without exception, the plantations depended on enslaved Africans to work the sugarcane fields. Sugar, once an expensive novelty, was now considered a necessity in the European diet.

The plantation system was so successful for sugarcane that it spread to other crops. By 1800, plantations were well

Boiling cane juice into syrup.

established in the southern areas of North America, where enslaved Africans were forced to work long hours in cotton and tobacco fields.

Slavery and the Middle Passage

Along with European demand for more sugar came plantation owners' need for more slaves. Providing slaves to the Caribbean became a big business in itself. For nearly 400 years, enslaved Africans were brought to the Americas. Most came between 1700 and 1800, when European demand for sugar was greatest. Most stayed in the Caribbean, with only about one in twenty going to cotton and tobacco plantations in America's southern colonies.

European and later American slavers sailed to Africa where they arranged with African slavers to capture African men, women, and some children. In the early 1500s, Africans lived in many different tribes that often waged war against one another. Victorious tribes enslaved members of losing tribes. These African slavers forced hundreds of thousands of Africans from central and western Africa to march west to African seaports, where they were sold to European or American slavers.

Slaves often were branded with a red-hot branding iron to mark them as slaves and identify their new owners. They were herded onto slave ships, chained in pairs, and packed between the decks. The space allowed was not high enough for them to stand up.

The 4,000-mile sea voyage from West Africa to the Caribbean was called the *Middle Passage* because it was the second stage or passage in a three-stage journey. In the first stage, Africans became enslaved in Africa; in the third, they were sent throughout the Caribbean. The second-stage trip of many weeks was a nightmare come to life. Some slaves jumped overboard, preferring to die rather than live enslaved. Others choked themselves to death with their chains. Many died from disease or from eating rotten food.

The trip's end in the Caribbean did not mean the end of brutal and inhumane treatment. Often shiploads of slaves were taken to central locations on the islands where they were "seasoned." Seasoning included brutal whippings and other harsh punishments calculated to remove any trace of rebellion or resistance. Once a slave was considered properly seasoned, he or she was ready for the plantation fields.

The Triangular Trades

By 1700, Europeans had developed regular trade routes among traders in the Americas, Europe, and Africa. Because the patterns made by cargo ships created giant triangles across the Atlantic Ocean, the routes came to be known as the *triangular trades.*

Slavers had several triangular routes. On one such route, ships from Europe transported manufactured goods to Africa's west coast. There the goods were exchanged for slaves. The slaves were carried across the Atlantic Ocean to the West Indies, where they were sold at a huge profit. The slavers then used that profit to buy sugar, coffee, and tobacco to take back to Europe.

Another triangular trade route began in New England harbors, where ships filled with rum and other products set sail for Africa. At West African ports, the New England cargoes were traded for slaves, who then were transported to the Caribbean. There they were sold to plantation owners in exchange for molasses, which was taken to the rum producers in New England.

In the 1700s, one of the quickest ways to make a fortune was to engage in triangular trades. One authority reports that in slave trade alone profits from buying slaves in Africa and selling them in the Caribbean could exceed 700 percent!

Two Triangular Trades. Slave traders made huge profits transporting slaves and goods across the ocean.

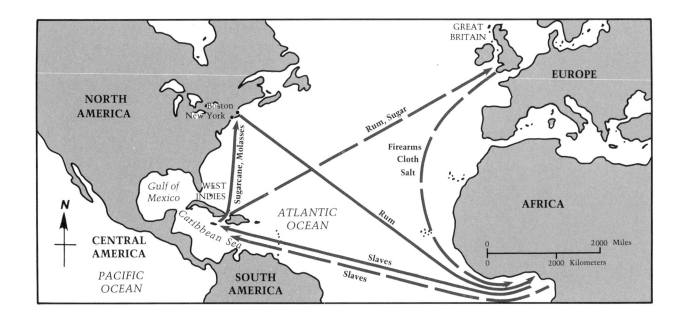

Slave Life

On Monday through Saturday, plantation slaves had to report to work before dawn. They worked in fields or sugar processing plants and as craftspersons, animal tenders, and household servants. They were allowed half an hour for breakfast at 9 a.m., had some time for a midday meal, then worked until dark. Many plantation owners treated their enslaved workers very cruelly, feeding them little and whipping them often. Members of slave families were often separated and sold, and never rejoined. Even the kindest owners took from the slaves their most important right—freedom.

During the little time they had off, the Caribbean slaves planted and cared for their own gardens, worked on their living quarters, or practiced crafts such as basket weaving and pottery making. Some slaves became so successful with their gardens and crafts that they developed their own markets. They traded among themselves and even sold goods and foods to the plantation owners.

Caribbean slaves also acquired sophisticated knowledge about the natural environment of the islands. They followed some of the farming and medical practices of island Indians, such as the use of native plants for food and medicine. When possible, they also applied knowledge from their African heritage to their new environment.

Perhaps the first contribution that enslaved Africans freely made to the Americas was their knowledge of ways to prepare a wide variety of vegetables, fruits, meats, and fish. Using the African way of seasoning food with spices and herbs, slaves experimented with the spices available in the Americas. They also learned that adding vegetables to starchy meals of corn meal and beans made their daily diets more nutritious.

After Slavery

After 1800, the Caribbean sugarcane industry went into slow decline. During the century, wars in Europe caused a drop in sugar demand and German and French farmers began to grow sugar beets. By the late 1800s, production of sugar from sugar beets exceeded that of sugarcane. Slavery was gradually abolished in the Americas, and in 1888, Brazil became the last country in the Americas to outlaw slavery.

Since slavery's official end, people of African descent in the Americas have struggled to gain full equality and just treatment. Today, some descendants of African slaves in the Caribbean still produce sugar at far below average wages. African Americans in the United States are still fighting to attain equality in education and jobs and to become equal participants in our democracy.

The one positive note in the sad history of sugar is the remarkable survival and adaptation of enslaved Africans. Thousands of these forced migrants stayed alive despite the brutality of their work. They adapted to a new environment with great skill. Unlike many plantation owners, African slaves learned to use the land and plants of the Caribbean and southern colonies to their advantage. They improved their own lives and shared their knowledge with immigrants to the Americas who came after them.

African contributions to world cultures have been significant. African contributions to food, art, music, writing, religion, and community life enrich the lives of people throughout the Americas and the world.

The Nature of Slavery

Frederick Douglass (c. 1818–1895) became a runaway slave in 1838. He committed his life to the fight for African American rights. Here he describes the legal relation of master and slave.

Frederick Douglass

"The law gives the master absolute power over the slave," Douglass wrote. "He may work him, flog him, hire him out, sell him, and, in certain contingencies, *kill* him, with perfect impunity [freedom from punishment]. The slave is a human being, divested of all rights—reduced to the level of a brute—a mere 'chattel' [property] in the eye of the law—placed beyond the circle of human brotherhood—cut off from his kind—his name, which the 'recording angel' may have enrolled in heaven, among the blest, is impiously [wickedly] inserted in a *master's ledger,* with horses, sheep, and swine. In law, the slave has no wife, no children, no country, and no home. He can own nothing, possess nothing, acquire nothing, but what must belong to another."

PLEASURE, PROFIT, AND SATIATION

Sidney W. Mintz

Sidney W. Mintz is an anthropologist at the Johns Hopkins University in Baltimore, Maryland. In his research, Dr. Mintz has analyzed the nature of human preference for sugar and traced the growth of the sugar industry worldwide. This excerpt is taken from Dr. Mintz's research and writing for the book, Seeds of Change, *published by the Smithsonian Institution Press.*

Without the human liking for the taste of sweetness, sugar never could have acquired its past and present importance. If not universal, that liking is at least extremely widespread. Science has not succeeded entirely in explaining the seemingly universal human liking for the sweet taste. Human beings also like sour, bitter, salty, and other tastes. They can even learn to like such unusual tastes as that of hot peppers; of rotting food, such as cheese; or even of highly hazardous foods, such as mushrooms or the Japanese blowfish, fugu. Yet sweetness occupies a privileged place in the spectrum of human tastes. We know of no people who, once having eaten sweet foods, rejected them entirely. When such rejections have occurred, they have been linked to dieting or religious beliefs, to moral or self-improvement impulses of some kind—to a rejection of something *already* considered desirable. . . .

Before the processing of sucrose from plants into granular sugars had been developed, honey was the commonest of all sweeteners. . . . In the West, only after the appearance of partly crystallized sugar did honey begin to be supplanted as the sweetest of sweet foods.

Most of the sugar in honey is not sucrose but invert sugar, that is, levulose (fruit sugar) and dextrose (grape sugar). Though proportions are now changing, most sweet foods eaten in the world today are sweetened by sucrose, not other sugars.

The English were among the first Europeans to develop a strong liking for sugar. The English afternoon tea often included cakes and other sweet treats.

Sucrose is produced in green plants by photosynthesis in a complex series of reactions in which the energy of sunlight is absorbed by the chlorophyll of the leaves to convert carbon dioxide from the air and water from the soil into organic compounds, liberating oxygen in the process. Manufacture of sucrose and other carbohydrates by green plants is a vital part of the architecture of life on earth. Since these plants are food for much of the animal world, plants and animals stand in a strikingly interdependent relationship. The remarkable capacity of green plants to produce sugars and liberate oxygen is the obverse of human chemistry. In effect, we produce carbon dioxide and consume sugars; while green plants give off oxygen and produce sugars, and consume carbon dioxide.

Hence it cannot really be said that we humans *manufacture* sugar; we *extract* sucrose. While concentrating it and removing impurities, we change it to other states by a series of steps: separating from the plant fibers the juice containing the sucrose; cleaning the juice by adding substances to which foreign matter will adhere, then removing them; heating the liquid to reduce its volume and increase its density; and finally refining the syrup to produce a liquid or a solid sugar. Familiar granular white sugar is as pure chemically as anything we eat.

Sugarcane

Before about 1830, sugarcane was the most important sucrose-carrying plant used by human beings. It had been used to make partially crystallized sugar for at least fifteen hundred years. It still rules the world market for sucrose, though it has experienced periods of decline and has powerful rivals. The sugar beet is the other commercially important, worldwide source of sucrose. Sugar was extracted experimentally from the beet by the mid-eighteenth century, but beet sugar did not become commercially and economically practical until around 1830. Its importance in the New World is quite recent.

The story of sugarcane—and of cane sugar—is different. The sugarcane was first domesticated ten or twelve thousand years ago in New Guinea, only then diffusing to mainland Asia. Cane juice was probably not used to produce a solid substance until near the beginning of the Christian era. Between about 350 B.C. and A.D. 350, people succeeded in using controlled heat to turn the juice of the sugarcane into a taffy-like, partly crystalline solid—the first "sugar." This probably happened in Indo-Persian Khuzestan. From there, sugar and technical knowledge about its fabrication began to spread in every direction. . . .

Sugar in Europe

. . . The sugarcane and the technology of sucrose extraction and elaboration were part of the Islamic expansion, carried across North Africa by the Moors. They brought cane with them into Spain (in the late ninth or early tenth century) and grew it there, as far north as Valencia. The Moors also brought with them knowledge of sugar making. Sugar was made from cane juice in Spain no later than the early tenth century. . . .

Though small amounts of sugar reached western Europe before the Moorish invasion, we know only that it was used as a medicine and spice, rather than as a food or sweetener. Northern Europe's awakening appetite for sugar, beginning with the crusades around A.D. 1000, was fed at first by the Mediterranean plantations. But Spain and Portugal were fated to play a critical role in the spread of sugarcane and sugar technology.

In the fifteenth century, Spain and Portugal extended sugar production to the Atlantic islands, which included Portuguese São Tomé and Madeira and the Spanish Canary Islands. These islands had benign climates and fresh soils, better suited than the Iberian Peninsula to cane growing. But they were small and mountainous, and they never completely supplanted those older sugar-producing areas that had begun to supply Europe. Large-scale replacement of both the Mediterranean and the Atlantic island producers occurred after the Americas began to produce sugar.

THE MIDDLE PASSAGE

Edward Reynolds

In 1985, Edward Reynolds, Professor of History, University of California, San Diego, published Stand the Storm: A History of the Atlantic Slave Trade. *The excerpt below describes the treatment of Africans during the horrendous journey from West Africa to the Caribbean. Included in the reading is a quotation from the slave Olaudah Equiano, whose autobiography was first published in 1798. Equiano was one of the few slaves who wrote their autobiographies.*

As you read:
• **Why do you think it was in the best interest of ship captains to be concerned about the diet and health of the slaves?**

A few days before embarking on the ships, all slaves—male and female—had their heads shaved. When the cargo belonged to several owners, differentiating brands had to be impressed on the bodies of the Africans, using pieces of silver wire or small irons fashioned into the owner's initials. Portuguese traders baptized their slaves before transporting them, since it was forbidden under pain of excommunication to carry any slaves to Brazil who had not been christened. . . .

There are few personal accounts describing the emotions of those who were placed on board the slave ships. Olaudah Equiano is one who has left us his reaction to this experience:

The first object which saluted my eyes when I arrived on the coast was the sea, and a slave ship which was then riding at anchor and waiting for its cargo. These filled me with astonishment, which was soon converted into terror when I was carried on board. I was immediately handled and tossed up to see if I were sound by some of the crew, and I was now persuaded that I had gotten into a world of bad spirits and that they were going to kill me. Their complexions too differing so much from ours, their hair and the language they spoke (which was very different from any I had ever heard) united to confirm me in this belief. Indeed such were the horrors of my views and fears at the moment that, if ten thousand worlds had been my own, I would have

The cruelties of slavery began in Africa, where slavers marched captives to western ports for sale.

freely parted with them all to have exchanged my condition with that of the meanest slave in my own country. When I looked around the ship too and saw a large furnace of copper boiling, and a multitude of black people of every description chained together, every one of their countenances [faces] expressing dejection and sorrow, I no longer doubted of my fate; and quite overpowered with horror and anguish, I fell motionless on the deck and fainted.[1]

Most slaves understandably showed extreme distress and despair at being torn away from their homeland and dread of what came to be known as the Middle Passage. Some feared that they were being taken away to be eaten by their captors; the attempts by some slavers to explain to the victims the purpose for which they had been purchased failed to allay their fears. . . .

Slaves were brought up on deck at eight o'clock in the morning. Their irons were examined and a long chain locked to a ring fixed in the deck was run through the rings of the shackles of the men and locked to another ring-bolt fixed in the deck. In this way, sixty or more slaves could be fastened to the chains to prevent attempts at rebellion. They were given water with which to wash, and the ship's surgeon then examined them for sores or other ailments. Those who were ill were taken to a special section of the boat where they were treated.

Meals were served twice daily: breakfast around ten a.m. and another meal at four in the afternoon. The diet usually included rice, farina, yams and horse beans [broad beans]; on rare occasions, bran might be included. Some slavers offered their captives a so-called "African meal" once a day, followed in the evening by a European meal which consisted of horse beans boiled into a pulp. Most African slaves hated this dish so much that they would throw it overboard unless closely watched while eating. . . .

In order to control the hungry captives' food consumption the process of eating was sometimes directed by signals from a monitor, who indicated when the slaves should dip their fingers or wooden spoons into the food and when they should swallow. It was the responsibility of the monitor to report those who refused to eat, and any slaves found to be attempting to starve themselves were severely whipped. There were instances in which hot coals were put on a shovel and placed so near the lips of a recalcitrant [stubborn] slave that his mouth was scorched

A slave ship of the 1700s.

SEEDS • OF • CHANGE

and burned. At other times, the *speculum orum*, a mouth opener, was used to force food down a slave's throat. . . .

The prevalence of disease at sea required that captains maintain some measure of cleanliness and employ a ship's surgeon. Slave cargoes were afflicted by fevers, dysentery and smallpox—smallpox being particularly disastrous, since there was no cure. At intervals, the slaves had their mouths rinsed with vinegar or lime juice, and were given a dram of the juice as an antidote to scurvy. To these health dangers were added the torments of seasickness and the oppressive heat in the holds. Ventilation was provided by about half a dozen portholes on either side of the ship. The hatches and bulkheads of slaving ships had grates, with openings cut above the deck for ventilation. When stifling tropical air in the hold made ventilation difficult at night, the gratings were removed and some of the slaves were allowed on the deck. In rainy weather when the gratings were covered, the slaves nearly suffocated.

Sick slaves were often placed under the half-deck where they slept on planks. At dawn, the surgeon would frequently find several slaves dead, still fastened to the living by their leg-irons. The practice of throwing dead slaves overboard brought sharks from miles around to feed on the bodies. Those slaves lacking the will to live often found ways to end their agonies. Women used cotton skirts as rope with which to hang themselves; other slaves jumped overboard when sentries were not vigilant.

The fear of slave mutinies led to strict controls, and intractable captives were severely punished. Although all would have welcomed the opportunity to escape, slaves from certain areas earned a reputation for rebellion. The so-called "Coromantees" of the Gold Coast were particularly known for their pride and mutinous behaviour. . . . Often, the slaves sought to kill the European traders and set the vessel ashore. Slavers went to great lengths to prevent rebellions and mutinies, visiting the holds daily and searching every corner between decks for pieces of iron, wood or knives gathered by the slaves. Great care was taken not to leave lying about any object that could be used as a weapon. The yearning of slaves for their homelands led inevitably to rebellious attempts to gain liberty.

An advertisement for "healthy" slaves.

A SLAVER'S LOG BOOK

Captain Theophilus Conneau

Captain Tehophilus Conneau was a slaver, a person who bought, transported, and sold slaves. Writing in the 1820s, Conneau's log book includes a description of the landing and sale of slave cargo.

As you read:
- **What feelings and beliefs about Africans are evident in Conneau's writing?**
- **What methods did a plantation owner use to try to convince Africans of the advantages of being a white man's slave?**

As I have fully described the mode of shipping, feeding, sleeping, and securing of the slaves on ship board, I shall next narrate the manner they are landed in the Island of Cuba. But before I do so, let me crave the indulgence of the reader if I again correct many remarks made by public newspapers and pamphlets on the filthy condition that slaves are forced to be subjected to during the middle passage. I have said before that slaves are stripped and kept naked for the sole object of cleanliness; I have also described the policy of the slaver in regard to washing and scraping of the slave deck. Let me further inform the reader that whenever the weather permits, they are also made to bathe, and it's invariably done once a week. . . .

Once the cargo is landed, it is hastened in the Interior as soon as possible, escorted by the Captain and part of the crew all well armed, and made to walk at a rapid rate. In this manner they are conducted to the nearest plantation whose consent is purchased before, and there disposed, mentioning the nation but not the owner, Captain, or the vessel. . . .

Messengers are sent off to the different slave brokers, who inform the needy purchaser that a quantity of Bossal [the name of a place in central Africa] slaves are to be disposed. . . .

On the arrival of the slaves in a plantation, they are well fed with fresh provisions and abundance of fruit, which greatly astonishes the African who in his joy forgets his country, friends, and relations. But his wonder rests not there. The new clothes, the red cap, and the blanket (a civilized superfluity not yet accustomed to) dumbs him with surprise. . . . The arrival of a carriage or cart creates no little confusion on this benighted [backward] Ethiopian, who has no idea that animals can be

SEEDS • OF • CHANGE

made to work, and in his African ignorance admires the white man's ingenuity.

But the grand demonstration of the surprise of surprises is at hand: a Black postillion [horse-mounted guide] in his red jacket and silver spurs alights from a prancing horse and in the language of their mothers bids them welcome and in the name of Allah [the Moslem name for God] blesses their safe arrival. A furor takes place. Every African wishes to embrace and snap fingers with the equestrian civilized African brother, who by his Master's order preaches them a well-learnt sermon of the happiness of being a white man's slave, cracking his whip on the well-polished boot to enforce his untruthful arguments.

The slave deck of the Wildfire, *on its way to the Caribbean in the 1800s.*

THE HISTORY OF MARY PRINCE

(Related by herself.)

Very few writings by enslaved people in the Caribbean exist. Those stories we know about were often told to and recorded by others. In The History of Mary Prince, a West Indian Slave, *published in 1831, Mary Prince tells of her life as a slave. The series of excerpts that follows relates a tale of cruelty, suffering, and courage.*

As you read:
- **If you were to describe the nature of slavery based on this reading, what would you say?**
- **How do you think Mary Prince would have responded to the argument that slaves were essential to the success of the plantation system?**

I was born at Brackish-Pond, in Bermuda, on a farm belonging to Mr. Charles Myners. My mother was a household slave; and my father, whose name was Prince, was a sawyer [a person who saws wood] belonging to Mr. Trimmingham, a ship-builder at Crow-Lane. When I was an infant, old Mr. Myners died, and there was a division of the slaves and other property among the family. I was bought along with my mother by old Captain Darrel, and given to his grandchild, little Miss Betsey Williams. Captain Williams, Mr. Darrel's son-in-law, was master of a vessel which traded to several places in America and the West Indies, and he was seldom at home long together.

Mrs. Williams was a kind-hearted good woman, and she treated all her slaves well. She had only one daughter, Miss Betsey, for whom I was purchased, and who was about my own age. I was made quite a pet of by Miss Betsey, and loved her very much. She used to lead me about by the hand, and call me her little nigger. This was the happiest period of my life; for I was too young to understand rightly my condition as a slave, and too thoughtless and full of spirits to look forward to the days of toil and sorrow.

My mother was a household slave in the same family. I was under her own care, and my little brothers and sisters were my play-fellows and companions. My mother had several fine children after she came to Mrs. Williams,—three girls and two boys. The tasks given out to us children were light, and we

SEEDS • OF • CHANGE

used to play together with Miss Betsey, with as much freedom almost as if she had been our sister.

My master, however, was a very harsh, selfish man; and we always dreaded his return from sea. His wife was herself much afraid of him; and, during his stay at home, seldom dared to show her usual kindness to the slaves. . . .

After Mrs. Williams died, Mary Prince was to be sold, along with two of her sisters. Mary's family would be separated forever.

The black morning at length came; it came too soon for my poor mother and us. Whilst she was putting on us the new osnaburgs [rough cotton fabric] in which we were to be sold, she said, in a sorrowful voice, (I shall never forget it!) "See, I am *shrouding* my poor children; what a task for a mother!" . . .

We followed my mother to the market-place, where she placed us in a row against a large house, with our backs to the wall and our arms folded across our breasts. I, as the eldest, stood first, Hannah next to me, then Dinah; and our mother stood beside, crying over us. My heart throbbed with grief and terror so violently, that I pressed my hands quite tightly across by breast, but I could not keep it still, and it continued to leap as though it would burst out of my body. But who cared for that? Did one of the many by-standers, who were looking at us so carelessly, think of the pain that wrung the hearts of the negro woman and her young ones? No, no! They were not all bad, I dare say, but slavery hardens white people's hearts towards the blacks; and many of them were not slow to make their remarks upon us aloud, without regard to our grief— though their light words fell like cayenne [hot red pepper] on the fresh wounds of our hearts. Oh those white people have small hearts who can only feel for themselves.

At length the vendue [auction] master, who was to offer us for sale like sheep or cattle, arrived, and asked my mother which was the eldest. She said nothing, but pointed to me. He took me by the hand, and led me out into the middle of the street, and, turning me slowly round, exposed me to the view of those who attended the vendue. I was soon surrounded by strange men, who examined and handled me in the same manner that a butcher would a calf or a lamb he was about to purchase, and who talked about my shape and size in like words—as if I could no more understand their meaning than

Plantation owners look over a slave for sale at an auction.

the dumb beasts. I was then put up to sale. The bidding commenced at a few pounds [British units of money], and gradually rose to fifty-seven, when I was knocked down to the highest bidder; and the people who stood by said that I had fetched a great sum for so young a slave.

I then saw my sisters led forth, and sold to different owners; so that we had not the sad satisfaction of being partners in bondage. When the sale was over, my mother hugged and kissed us, and mourned over us, begging of us to keep up a good heart, and do our duty to our new masters. It was a sad parting; one went one way, one another, and our poor mammy went home with nothing.

Mary Prince's new masters were very cruel, often inflicting very brutal punishment.

I got a sad fright, that night. I was just going to sleep, when I heard a noise in my mistress's room; and she presently called out to inquire if some work was finished that she had ordered Hetty [a household slave] to do. "No, Ma'am, not yet," was Hetty's answer from below. On hearing this, my master started up from his bed, and just as he was, in his shirt, ran down stairs with a long cow-skin [a hard twisted cowhide whip] in his hand. I heard immediately after, the cracking of the thong, and the house rang to the shrieks of poor Hetty, who kept crying out, "Oh, Massa! Massa! me dead. Massa! have mercy upon me—don't kill me outright."—This was a sad beginning for me. I sat up upon my blanket, trembling with terror, like a frightened hound, and thinking that my turn would come next. At length the house became still, and I forgot for a little while all my sorrows by falling fast asleep. . . .

After being sold a second time, Mary Prince and other slaves were subjected to continuing cruelties.

Though we worked from morning till night, there was no satisfying Mr. D——. I hoped, when I left Capt. I——, that I should have been better off, but I found it was but going from one butcher to another. There was this difference between them: my former master used to beat me while raging and foaming with passion; Mr. D—— was usually quite calm. He would stand by and give orders for a slave to be cruelly whipped, and assist in the punishment, without moving a muscle of his face; walking about and taking snuff [powdered tobac-

A field hand.

SEEDS • OF • CHANGE

co] with the greatest composure. Nothing could touch his hard heart—neither sighs, nor tears, nor prayers, nor streaming blood; he was deaf to our cries, and careless of our sufferings. Mr. D—— has often . . . hung me up by the wrists, and beat me with the cow-skin, with his own hand, till my body was raw with gashes. Yet there was nothing very remarkable in this; for it might serve as a sample of the common usage of the slaves on that horrible island. . . .

Mr. D—— had a slave called old Daniel, whom he used to treat in the most cruel manner. Poor Daniel was lame in the hip, and could not keep up with the rest of the slaves; and our master would order him to be stripped and laid down on the ground, and have him beaten with a rod of rough briar till his skin was quite red and raw. He would then call for a bucket of salt, and fling upon the raw flesh till the man writhed on the ground like a worm, and screamed aloud with agony. . . .

Mary Prince eventually married, but she remained separated from her husband. She was taken to England and won her freedom there. In the final excerpt below, she comments on the institution of slavery.

The man that says slaves be quite happy in slavery—that they don't want to be free—that man is either ignorant or a lying person. I never heard a slave say so. I never heard a Buckra [white] man say so, till I heard tell of it in England. Such people ought to be ashamed of themselves. They can't do without slaves, they say. What's the reason they can't do without slaves as well as in England? No slaves here—no whips—no stocks—no punishment, except for wicked people. They hire servants in England; and if they don't like them, they send them away: they can't lick them. Let them work ever so hard in England, they are far better off than slaves. If they get a bad master, they give warning and go hire to another. They have their liberty. That's just what we want. We don't mind hard work, if we had proper treatment, and proper wages like English servants, and proper time given in the week to keep us from breaking the Sabbath. But they won't give it: they will have work—work—work, night and day, sick or well, till we are quite done up; and we must not speak up nor look amiss, however much we be abused. And then when we are quite done up, who cares for us, more than for a lame horse? This is slavery. I tell it to let the English people know the truth. . . .

ONE WORLD

CHOOSING A POSITIVE FUTURE

The Columbus voyages triggered a 500-year period of exchanges between two old, well-established worlds. You have learned about five "seeds" that caused significant changes in both worlds. Some of the changes were positive, others were negative.

The introduction of maize and potatoes to the people of Europe resulted in generally positive changes, although the Irish potato famine caused great suffering. In Africa, however, maize became a basic food on the slave ships. Both maize and potatoes have become staples throughout the world. They have supported population growth, saved millions of Africans and Europeans from possible starvation, and fueled Europe's Industrial Revolution. Disease and sugarcane had

negative results. Smallpox and other diseases reduced the American Indian population by as much as 90 percent. The introduction of sugarcane led to the enslavement of millions of Africans. The return of the horse to the Americas had both negative and positive consequences. Horses first aided the Spanish in their conquest of the Americas and then significantly changed the cultures of many American Indian tribes.

The earth viewed from the moon.

The Human Exchange

Thousands of other exchanges producing equally widespread and far-reaching consequences have occurred since 1492. One of the most important exchanges has been the massive human immigration to the Americas during

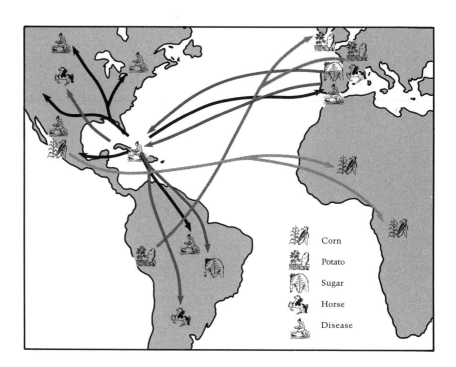

Corn	
Potato	
Sugar	
Horse	
Disease	

The Five Seeds of Change

the past 500 years. More than fifty million Europeans immigrated to the Americas between 1600 and 1900. More than ten million Africans came unwillingly to the Americas. The majority came during the 1700s, when the demand for sugar in Europe was at its highest. Beginning in the mid-1800s, thousands of Asians joined the flood of immigrants to the Americas.

Immigration and high birth rates led to a population explosion in the Americas. The current population of North and South America exceeds 725 million and is growing rapidly. For example, experts estimate that the population of all the countries south of the United States will double by the year 2023, reaching almost one billion.

Immigration to the Americas has resulted in a *multicultural population,* one made up of people from many different races and cultures. Our skin colors and physical features vary widely. We live in many different countries under different forms of government. We speak many different languages and dialects, practice scores of different religions, and engage in many kinds of jobs and professions. We enjoy different kinds of music, art, literature, and other cultural activities. Although conflicts sometimes arise from this cultural intermixture, the merging of people's skills, ideas, and beliefs has created vigorous, dynamic societies. These societies offer the world a richness in variety similar to the variety that existed in American Indian societies 500 years ago.

The Human Impact on Nature

A negative consequence of population growth and economic development has been the impact on our natural environment. The 725 million people in the Americas and the remaining 4.5 billion people worldwide must be fed, clothed, and housed. To meet their needs, people, no matter where they live, use natural resources—land, plants, animals, water, forests, minerals, and air.

Europeans who first saw the Americas returned to their countries with tales of lands overflowing with seemingly limitless resources. Immigrants to the Americas and their descendants used natural resources with little thought of the long-term consequences. Trappers and hunters destroyed wildlife and extinguished many species, such as the passenger pigeon. Other species have been brought to the brink of extinction—the beaver, buffalo, bald eagle, and wild turkey, for example. Experts estimate that at least 400 animal species that existed 500 years ago are now extinct.

In North America, settlers, pioneers, and loggers have cut down forests that once stretched along both coasts, destroying in the process the habitat of many plant and wildlife species. Farmers and ranchers turned the vast grasslands of the Great Plains into "America's breadbasket," which fed millions but now needs continual nutrient replacement with fertilizers.

In South America, precious rain forests have been and are being cut down by the hundreds of thousands of acres every year. Animal species are lost before they are discovered, and plants that might produce cures for AIDS and cancer are being destroyed.

Multiplier Effect

Each destructive change has caused a *multiplier effect.* That is, a small change multiplies many times over before its impact stops. With the forests and grasses of the Great Plains gone, erosion occurs because root systems to anchor the soil have disappeared. Insecticides to destroy pests and fertilizers to replenish the soil have caused pollution of rivers, lakes, and oceans.

Cities and towns now sprawl across land where American Indian villages once stood. Exhaust from motor vehicles creates poisonous gases called *smog.* Emissions from factory and power plant smokestacks are responsible for *acid rain,* polluted rain that destroys lakes, forests, rivers, and crops. People throughout the Americas add their own personal pollution by carelessly throwing away used plastic, glass, and paper on the land or in waterways and oceans. Our use of chlorofluorocarbons (CFCs) in aerosol propellants, air conditioning units, and cleaning fluids is destroying the ozone layer in our atmosphere, which protects our planet from the sun's harmful ultraviolet rays.

On our planet, we have no "new worlds" left. We can no longer escape to a new, safe place. While the population of the Americas has been growing, so have the populations of other continents. Since 1492, the world's population has increased from 400 million to over 5 billion people today. Estimates are that the world's consumers, led by those in the United States and Europe, will use so much oil and natural gas that the world will run out of known supplies of these resources in less than 35 years. The wasteful use of resources has put nature, as well as humankind, at serious risk.

An Interdependent World

Despite the diversities of cultures and beliefs, the world's people are *interdependent.* They rely on each other. Wheat from Canada and the United States feeds people in Eastern Europe. Europeans and North Americans depend on Mexican and Middle Eastern oil. Modern transportation carries people and products from city to city, country to country, and continent to continent. Day and night, communication satellites link people together with ideas and news. Rapid transportation and communication have aided leaders of the world's nations in promoting peace.

If interdependence brings us many benefits, it also brings us responsibilities. Each of us is responsible for protecting our planet. Earth has only one atmosphere, and its oceans are all connected. Air pollution in one part of the world or toxic waste dumped in one ocean can soon affect other parts of the globe. We all share in nature's gifts, and we must also share the responsibility for nature's destruction and pollution.

Many of the products we use and then carelessly discard can harm wildlife.

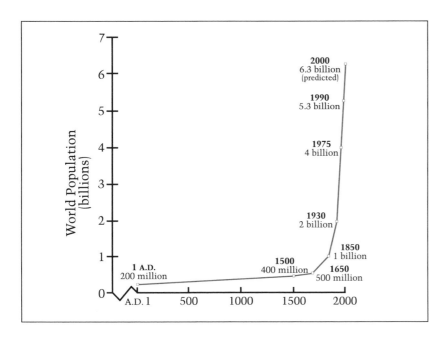

***World Population Growth,
A.D. 1 to 2000.*** *Today, the
world's population is thirteen
times greater than it was in
1492. It could reach ten billion by 2035. Scientists are
concerned that the earth cannot supply enough food to feed
ten billion people.*

Choosing a Positive Future

To reduce the environmental threat, we need to become
aware of our past mistakes and turn our awareness into
action to stop our environment's destruction. Such action is
beginning. Concerned people have helped limit human use
of parks and wilderness areas. Others have worked to clean
up lakes, rivers, and beaches. Some work to pass laws protecting endangered plants, wildlife, and wilderness. Some
write books and magazine articles, appear on TV, and visit
community groups and schools. Their purpose is to educate
people about environmental dangers that exist and the
methods available to avoid those dangers. Scientists and
doctors study and experiment with our natural resources,
hoping to find solutions to problems such as widespread
famine in Africa and Asia and the growing threats of two
diseases, AIDS and cancer.

Much more needs to be done. We must realize that all natural resources are limited and acknowledge that nature needs
time and care to renew and heal itself. We can demand fewer
things such as cars and TV sets. We can use less electricity,
walk more often instead of ride, and conserve fresh water. By
reducing our wants, we can help nature rest and start to preserve our planet for ourselves and coming generations.

Nature's survival requires us to rethink our attitudes. We
must practice the three Rs—recycle, reuse, and reduce. We

must decide that future development be *sustainable development*—development that will protect the environment, yet provide for all the earth's living things.

We must find ways to feed the world's starving populations, to help people in less-developed countries attain a better standard of living, and to maintain the living standards of developed countries. We must do all these things without further polluting our air and water, depleting our rain forests, or destroying the fragile ozone layer. Otherwise, the slow destructive process that has begun will speed up, creating even more alarming environmental consequences.

One World

In 1492, two old but very different worlds existed. When Columbus landed in the Caribbean, he triggered a series of changes and exchanges that have made one world from those two old worlds. Exchanges and changes will continue to occur. The processes of change and exchange in the past 500 years mean that we now live in one world—a very small one. As we plant seeds of change for the future, we must do so with a concern for all people and for the environment we all share. Our small planet is groaning under the load of trying to meet the wants and needs of all who live on it. Only by working together as individuals and as groups can we renew our planet and ourselves. Our challenge is global, and the choices belong to each of us.

Learning from Ancient Farmers

To meet human needs while preserving natural resources is the challenge of sustainable development. The International Potato Institute in Peru is sponsoring research that reconstructs the ways ancient farmers grew potatoes. The research may be one step toward sustainable development in South America.

Near Lake Titicaca in Bolivia, modern-day farmers discovered a 3,000-year-old system of canals and raised fields. After restoring the ancient farming system, the farmers discovered that pre-Incan and Incan methods produced seven times more potatoes than modern methods.

Peruvian terrace farm.

NOTES AND CREDITS

Readings Notes

Chapter 2, Conquistadors and Disease, pp. 29–31
[1]Henry F. Dobyns, "An Outline of Andean Epidemic History to 1720," *Bulletin of the History of Medicine* 37 (November–December 1963): 514. [2]Hans Staden, *The True History of His Captivity*, trans. Malcolm Letts (New York: Robert M. McBride and Co., 1929), 85–89. [3]David B. Quinn, ed., *The Roanoke Voyages* (London: The Hakluyt Society, 1955), 1:378. [4]Ibid. [5]Quoted in Alfred G. Bailey, *The Conflict of European and Eastern Algonkian Cultures, 1504–1700: A Study in Canadian Civilization* (St. John: New Brunswick Museum, 1937), 13. [6]Charles Francis Adams, *Three Episodes of Massachusetts History* (New York: Russell and Russell, 1965), 1:1–12.

Chapter 6, The Middle Passage, pp. 107-108
[1]Olaudah, Equiano, *Interesting Narrative of the Life of Olaudah Equiano, or Gustavus Vassa, the African, Written by Himself* (London, 1798; ed. Paul Edwards, Heinemann, 1967).

Reading Credits

Chapter 2
pp. 25–26: "Health Profiles," by John W. Verano and Douglas H. Ubelaker, Reprinted by permission of the Smithsonian Institution Press from *Seeds of Change: A Quincentennial Commemoration*, edited by Herman J. Viola and Carolyn Margolis. ©Smithsonian Institution 1991, pp. 222-223. **pp. 29–31:** Alfred W. Crosby, Jr., "Conquistador y Pestilencia: The First New World Pandemic and the Fall of the Great Indian Empires," *Hispanic American Historical Review*, v. 47:3, pp. 321–327. Copyright 1967, Duke University Press, Durham, North Carolina. Reprinted by permission of the publisher.

Chapter 3
pp. 41–44: "Thank the American Indian" by Herbert J. Spinden, *Scientific American*, vol. 138, April 1928, pp. 330–332. Reprinted with permission. Copyright ©1928 by Scientific American, Inc. All rights reserved. **pp. 47–49:** *Royal Commentaries of the Incas and General History of Peru, Part I* by Garcilaso de la Vega, translated by Harold V. Livermore. Austin: University of Texas Press, 1966, pp. 498–500. ©University of Texas Press. Reprinted by permission of the publisher. **pp. 50–51:** "The Strange Origin of Corn." *Journal of American Folklore.* 3(1890): pp.213–214. **pp. 52–53:** *Singing Valleys: The Story of Corn* by Dorothy Giles. New York: Random House, 1940, pp. 138–141.

Chapter 4
pp. 61–64: "American Food Crops in the Old World" by William H. McNeill. Reprinted by permission of the Smithsonian Institution Press from *Seeds of Change: A Quincentennial Commemoration*, edited by Herman J.

Viola and Carolyn Margolis. ©Smithsonian Institution 1991. pp. 47–50. **pp. 65–66:** Excerpt from *The Great Hunger* by Cecil Woodham-Smith. Copyright ©1962 by Cecil Woodham-Smith. Reprinted by permission of Harper Collins Publishers. **pp. 67–68:** Excerpt from *Paddy's Lament: Ireland 1846–1847* by Thomas Gallagher and Michael Gallagher, reprinted by permission of Harcourt Brace Jovanovich, Inc. **pp. 69–73:** Reprinted with permission from the December 1976 *Reader's Digest*. Copyright ©1976 by The Reader's Digest Assn., Inc.

Chapter 5
pp. 83–85: *The Conquest of New Spain* by Bernal Díaz, translated by J.M. Cohen (Penguin Classics, 1963) copyright ©J.M. Cohen, 1963. **pp. 86–87:** *Royal Commentaries of the Incas and General History of Peru, Part I*, by Garcilaso de la Vega, translated by Harold V. Livermore. Austin: University of Texas Press, 1966, pp. 579–582. Reprinted by permission of the publisher. **pp. 88–91:** Reprinted by permission of the Smithsonian Institution Press from *After Columbus: The Smithsonian Chronicle of the North American Indians*, by Herman J. Viola. ©Smithsonian Institution 1990. **p. 92:** Reprinted from *The Winged Serpent: An Anthology of American Prose and Poetry*, edited by Margot Astrov. New York: John Day Co. ©1946. Reprinted by permission of the editor. **pp. 93–95:** Reprinted from *A Bride Goes West* by Nannie T. Alderson and Helena Huntington Smith, by permission of University of Nebraska Press. Original copyright ©1942 by Farrar & Rinehart, Inc.

Chapter 6
pp. 104–106: "Pleasure, Profit, and Satiation," by Sidney W. Mintz. Reprinted by permission of the Smithsonian Institution Press from *Seeds of Change: A Quincentennial Commemoration*, edited by Herman J. Viola and Carolyn Margolis. ©Smithsonian Institution 1991. pp. 115–117. **pp. 107–109:** *Stand the Storm: A History of the Atlantic Slave Trade* by Edward Reynolds, pp. 47–56. (W.H. Allen, 1985) Reprinted by permission of the publisher.

Photographic Credits

Chapter 1
p. 5: National Park Service, U.S. Department of the Interior, photo by Fred Mang, Jr.; p. 9: Museo Nacional de Antropologia Mexico; p. 10: from Guamán Pomade Ayala, *Nueva Cronica*, courtesy of Det Kongelige Bibliotek, Copenhagen; p. 12: National Maritime Museum, Greenwich, England; p. 16: Bill E. Hess/©National Geographic Society.

Chapter 2
p. 19: North Wind Picture Archives; p. 21: courtesy of the Peabody Museum, Harvard University; p. 23: Reprinted with permission from *Lienzo de Tlaxcala*, ©Ed Castle/courtesy of Smithsonian Institution; p. 24: North Wind Picture Archives; p. 26: Culver Pictures; p. 28: from

the *Florentine Codex*, courtesy of the Peabody Museum, Harvard University; p. 30: Smithsonian Institution, Photo No. 3438; p. 33: National Museum of American Art, Smithsonian Institution.

Chapter 3
p. 35: North Wind Picture Archives; p. 37: Jerry McElroy; p. 40: Jerry McElroy; p. 43: Dumbarton Oaks Research Library and Collections, Washington, D.C.; p. 46: North Wind Picture Archives; p. 48: from Guamán Poma de Ayala, *Nueva Cronica*, courtesy of Det Kongelige Bibliotek, Copenhagen; p. 51: Collection of Paul Weatherwax, courtesy of the American Heritage Picture Collection; p. 53: North Wind Picture Archives.

Chapter 4
p. 55: from Guamán Poma de Ayala, *Nueva Cronica*, courtesy of Det Kongelige Bibliotek, Copenhagen; p. 57: John Verano/pottery courtesy of National Museum of Natural History, Smithsonian Institution; p. 60: Jerry McElroy; p. 62: Bibliothèque Nationale, Paris; p. 64: North Wind Picture Archives; p. 66: The Illustrated London News, December 22, 1849. Courtesy of Harvard University Library; p. 68: courtesy of the Library of Congress; p. 73: The National Potato Board.

Chapter 5
p. 75: Bancroft Library, University of California, Berkeley; p. 79: North Wind Picture Archives; p. 81: National Park Service, U.S. Department of the Interior, photo by Fred Mang, Jr.; p. 82: courtesy of the Library of Congress; p. 84: North Wind Picture Archives; p. 87: Fernando Suárez Gonzáles/Archivo de Indias; p. 89: North Wind Picture Archives; p. 91: Tom McHugh/Photo Researchers; p. 94: courtesy of the Library of Congress; p. 95: courtesy of the Library of Congress.

Chapter 6
p. 97: North Wind Picture Archives; p. 99: North Wind Picture Archives; p. 103: National Archives Exhibit No. 55; p. 105: North Wind Picture Archives; p. 107: North Wind Picture Archives; p. 111: North Wind Picture Archives; p. 113: courtesy of the Library of Congress; p. 114: North Wind Picture Archives.

Chapter 7
p. 117: NASA; p. 120: Visuals Unlimited/Daniel Gotshall; p. 122: Chip Clark.

INDEX

126